COOK'S BOOK OF
Sauces

COOK'S BOOK OF
Sauces

100 FOOLPROOF RECIPES TO TRANSFORM AN EVERYDAY DISH INTO A FEAST, SHOWN STEP BY STEP IN MORE THAN 500 PHOTOGRAPHS

CHRISTINE FRANCE

southwater

This edition is published by Southwater, an imprint of Anness Publishing Ltd,
Hermes House, 88–89 Blackfriars Road, London SE1 8HA;
tel. 020 7401 2077; fax 020 7633 9499
www.southwaterbooks.com; www.annesspublishing.com

If you like the images in this book and would like to investigate using them
for publishing, promotions or advertising, please visit our website www.practicalpictures.com for
more information.

UK agent: The Manning Partnership Ltd;
tel. 01225 478444; fax 01225 478440; sales@manning-partnership.co.uk
UK distributor: Grantham Book Services Ltd;
tel. 01476 541080; fax 01476 541061; orders@gbs.tbs-ltd.co.uk
North American agent/distributor: National Book Network;
tel. 301 459 3366; fax 301 429 5746; www.nbnbooks.com
Australian agent/distributor: Pan Macmillan Australia;
tel. 1300 135 113; fax 1300 135 103; customer.service@macmillan.com.au
New Zealand agent/distributor: David Bateman Ltd;
tel. (09) 415 7664; fax (09) 415 8892

Publisher: Joanna Lorenz
Managing Editor: Helen Sudell
Project Editor: Simona Hill
Recipes by: Alex Barker, Angela Boggiano, Carla Capalbo, Jacqueline Clark, Carole Clements, Roz
Denny, Nicola Diggins, Tessa Evelegh, Joanna Farrow, Christine France, Silvana Franco, Shirley Gill,
Nicola Graimes, Juliet Harbutt, Christine Ingram, Peter Jordan, Soheila Kimberley, Ruby Le Bois,
Lesley Macklay, Sue Maggs, Maggie Mayhew, Sallie Morris, Janice Murfitt, Maggie Pannell, Louise
Pickford, Katherine Richmond, Laura Washburn, Steven Wheeler, Kate Whiteman and Jeni Wright.
Designer: Simon Wilder
Production Controller: Pirong Wang

ACKNOWLEDGEMENTS

Thanks to the following photographers: Karl Adamson, Edward Allwright,
David Armstrong, Steve Baxter, James Duncan, John Freeman, Michelle Garrett,
John Heseltine, Amanda Heywood, Janine Hosegood, Don Last, William Lingwood, Patrick
McLeavy, Michael Michaels, Thomas Odulate, Debbie Patterson
and Juliet Piddington.

PUBLISHER'S NOTE

ETHICAL TRADING POLICY

Because of our ongoing ecological investment programme, you, as our customer, can have the
pleasure and reassurance of knowing that a tree is being cultivated on your behalf to naturally
replace the materials used to make the book you are holding.
For further information about this scheme, go to www.annesspublishing.com/trees

Previously published as part of a larger volume, *A Cook's Encyclopedia of Sauces*

Main front cover image shows Béarnaise Sauce – for recipe, see page 53

NOTES

Bracketed terms are intended for American readers.
For all recipes, quantities are given in both metric and imperial measures and,
where appropriate, measures are also given in standard cups and spoons.
Follow one set, but not a mixture because they are not interchangeable.
Standard spoon and cup measures are level.
1 tsp = 5ml, 1 tbsp = 15ml, 1 cup = 250ml/8fl oz
Australian standard tablespoons are 20ml. Australian readers should use 3 tsp in place
of 1 tbsp for measuring small quantities of salt etc.
Medium (US large) eggs are used unless otherwise stated.

Contents

Introduction 6

Understanding the Basics 8

Classic Sauces 42

Sauces for Pasta Dishes 64

Sauces for Meat Dishes 86

Sauces for Fish Dishes 106

Sauces for Vegetarian Dishes 124

Sauces for Sweet Dishes 136

Index 158

Introduction

Exactly the right sauce, properly prepared, is what turns good food into a great dish. Famous chefs, from Antonin Carême in the 19th century to today's flamboyant television stars, all recognize the importance of perfect sauces and acknowledge a legacy, which extends from pesto to cranberry sauce.

This book is packed with recipes for every kind of sweet and savoury sauce, as well as helpful suggestions for serving them. It begins with a foundation of the classics, including the basic repertoire of many cuisines from around the world. Pasta sauces, deservedly, have a whole chapter devoted to them. Recipes range from simple and refreshing vegetable sauces to rich and creamy classics and also include some exciting and innovative ideas for livening up whatever pasta you have in your pantry.

There is more to meat and poultry than traditional gravy, and Sauces for Meat Dishes offers a fabulous choice of fresh and fruity, hot and spicy, and sweet and sour accompaniments. Sauces for Fish Dishes contains delicate and subtly flavoured sauces to complement white fish and rich, robust and lively sauces for those with a sophisticated palate. Sauces for Vegetarian Dishes range from substantial cheese-based accompaniments to light and airy sauces that demonstrate just how versatile vegetables can be. Finally, Sauces for Sweet Dishes provides a wealth of wonderful and astonishingly quick and simple ways to brighten up basics, such as ice cream, meringues and fresh fruit.

A comprehensive introduction offers helpful advice on basic ingredients and how best to use them, while a guide to equipment suggests ways of ensuring perfect results every time. However basic the ingredients in your refrigerator, you will always be able to produce something special.

Understanding the Basics

Whether you are a novice cook who wants to add interest and new flavours to weekday meals, or an expert who would like to broaden your culinary repertoire, understanding the basics of sauce making will provide a firm foundation for a lifetime of creative cooking. Many sauce-making ingredients such as flour and fat are basics in every kitchen. Adding just a few other well-chosen ingredients will provide you with a pantry from which to make a whole range of interesting and flavourful accompaniments to meals.

Sauce making doesn't require any specialist equipment, and much of what you already own will be sufficient, such as a selection of pans, bowls, whisks, ladles, sieves, weighing scales and measuring jugs or cups.

The following pages provide a brief explanation of the science behind a successful sauce – which flours to use for a smooth texture, which fats add the best flavour, how much and what type of liquid to use and how to infuse (steep) flavours. All the basic methods of sauce making are included from a classic white sauce to a rich roux and there are plenty of hints and tips to help you produce the best results.

Flours

There is a wide range of flours and thickening agents on the market. It is important to select the right product, since the choice of flour used for a sauce will determine not only the cooking method used, but the final texture and flavour of the finished sauce. These general guidelines should help remove any mystique involved.

PLAIN WHITE FLOUR

Also known as all-purpose flour, this is the standard choice for making roux-based sauces and gravies. Its fine, smooth texture combines easily with melted fat for a sauce with a roux base, so that when heated, the starch grains burst and cook, thickening the sauce liquid.

White flour usually contains 70–75 per cent of the wheatgrain. Most of the bran and wheatgerm have been removed during milling, leaving it almost white, so it is excellent for thickening white sauces. White flour is chemically bleached, making it pale in colour and therefore more suitable for white sauces than unbleached, stone-ground flours.

SELF-RAISING (SELF-RISING), STRONG AND SOFT FLOURS

These are flours designed for specific baking uses, not for sauces, but could be used in an emergency if you run out of plain flour. Self-raising flour has chemical agents added during milling which react with heat to make cake mixtures rise during cooking. Strong flour has a higher proportion of gluten, making it most suitable for bread making. Soft flours have a lower gluten content, and are designed for cakes and pastries, but they also make a good thickener for smooth sauces.

Below from left to right: Brown flour, wholemeal (whole-wheat) flour

Below: Sauce flour

WHOLEMEAL (WHOLE-WHEAT), WHEATMEAL AND BROWN FLOURS

These flours contain more of the bran and wheatgerm, between 80 and 90 per cent of the grain, which gives them a nutty flavour, coarse texture and a darker colour. Because of this, they are not usually chosen for making sauces, but if you don't mind the texture and colour, there's no reason why any of them should not be used for thickening sauces. The bonus is that they will add a little extra dietary fibre and nutrients.

SAUCE FLOUR

This flour has been recently introduced, and has a lower protein level than ordinary wheat flour, so that sauces made with it are less likely to go lumpy. It is designed specifically for making cooked white sauces and gravies. It is also a good choice for making healthier sauces, since it is suitable for those made by the all-in-one or blending method, in which no fat is used.

Below: Plain (all-purpose) flour

Below, clockwise from top left: Cornflour (cornstarch), custard powder, potato flour, arrowroot

CORNFLOUR (CORNSTARCH)

This fine ground maize flour is a gluten-free starch. It is light and smooth-textured, producing velvety-textured, lump-free sauces, usually made by the blending method. When first added to a clear liquid it gives a cloudy appearance, but on heating, the sauce becomes almost clear. Because of this, it is a popular choice for Chinese sauces, and its smooth texture makes it particularly suitable for using in sweet white sauces or those that are to be used for coating foods.

POTATO FLOUR

Also known as farine de fécule, potato flour is made from pure potato starch. It is very fine and smooth and is bright white in colour. It makes a light, clear thickener for sauces without affecting the flavour. You will need slightly less potato flour than plain (all-purpose) flour for thickening. It is most suited to the blending method of sauce making, and is often used as a thickener in Chinese and Asian dishes and stir-fry sauces, so it is easily available from Asian stores.

ARROWROOT

This is a finely ground powder made from the root of a tropical tree, which is grown in Central America. It is used in the same way as cornflour, for sauces made by the blending method, and gives a very smooth, clear, translucent appearance to sweet or savoury sauces without affecting either the colour or the flavour.

CUSTARD POWDER

A useful store-cupboard (pantry) thickener for quick custard sauces, this is simply a coloured cornflour-based flour. For a quick custard, a similar result can be achieved by using a small amount of cornflour with a few drops of yellow food colouring and vanilla essence (extract). Make into a sauce with milk by the blending method, and sweeten to taste.

STORING FLOUR

Store flour in a cool, dark, dry, airy place, away from steam or damp. Place the flour into a clean tin or a storage jar with a close-fitting lid, and always make sure you wash and dry the container thoroughly before refilling it. Check the "use by" dates, and use up the flour within the recommended pack date, or replace it. Don't add new flour to old in a storage jar – it is always best to use up the older flour first.

Once opened, plain white flour can be stored under the right conditions for up to six months, but wholemeal (whole-wheat) and brown flours have a higher fat content so these are best used within two months.

Flour is best used while fresh. Make sure it is stored in dark, cool conditions; buy it in small quantities and plan to use it quickly rather than storing it indefinitely.

Fats

Fats make sauces palatable, and improve the flavour and texture. The ones usually used in sauces are "yellow" fats such as butter or margarine, or oils. Many are added to cooked sauces as a base with flour, as in a roux, or in beurre manié where the fat and flour are heated together to cook the starch grains for thickening. The classic emulsified sauces, such as hollandaise or mayonnaise, use either melted butter or liquid oils, beaten with eggs to enrich and thicken to a thick emulsion. The same principle is used in reduced sauces such as beurre blanc, or in oil-based salad dressings such as vinaigrette, where the fat is whisked into a reduced or well-flavoured liquid base to make a smooth emulsion. In salsas and purées, oil is added for flavour, being stirred or drizzled on to the ingredients.

TYPES OF FAT

Saturated fats are solid at room temperature, and are the ones that can raise cholesterol levels in the blood. Polyunsaturated fats can help lower cholesterol levels; mono-unsaturated fats, which are beneficial in regulating cholesterol levels, are liquid but can be made solid by a process known as hydrogenation. This is the process used to make margarines and spreads.

BUTTER

A natural product made by churning cream, butter has an 80 per cent fat content, which is saturated fat. Butter is made in two basic types, sweetcream and lactic, and both are available salted, lightly salted or unsalted (sweet). The choice will depend largely on flavour, according to whether you are making a sweet or savoury sauce.

Clockwise from top left: Ghee, clarified butter, concentrated butter

Clarified butter, ghee or concentrated butters will with-stand higher temperatures than untreated butter, and will not burn as easily.

MARGARINE

Soft (tub) margarines, made from a blend of vegetable oils and/or animal oils, have a soft, spreadable texture. Hard (packet) margarines have a firmer texture and are made from animal and vegetable fats. Both types have the same fat content as butter, and can be used as a direct substitute for butter in making sweet and savoury sauces. As the flavour is inferior to butter, margarines are best chosen for more robustly flavoured sauces where their own flavour will not be as noticeable.

Left: Lactic unsalted (sweet) butter (left), sweetcream salted butter

SPREADS

The wide choice of different spreads on the market is confusing to say the least, but as a rough guide, unless they are labelled "low-fat", or "very low-fat", they are generally suitable for sauce-making. After that, choice is very much a matter of personal preference.

Polyunsaturated vegetable oil spreads: Products described in this way are made either from a single vegetable oil or sunflower oil alone, or from a blend of different vegetable oils. They vary in fat content from 61 to 79 per cent.

Monounsaturated vegetable oil spreads: Made from olive oil or rapeseed (canola) oil, these vary in fat content from 60 to 75 per cent.

Dairy spreads: These contain cream or buttermilk to retain a buttery flavour and smooth texture, while providing a lower-fat alternative to butter. The fat content varies between 61 and 75 per cent.

Reduced fat spreads: These products are either made from vegetable oils alone or may also contain some dairy or animal fat. Their fat content is between 50 and 60 per cent.

Low-fat spreads and very low-fat spreads: These spreads, popular with the weight-conscious, contain less than 40 per cent fat, and are often as low as 25 per cent. They are not recommended for cooking, although they can be added to all-in-one method sauces.

Above, from left: Polyunsaturated, olive, dairy, and reduced-fat spreads

STORING FAT

All solid fats should be stored in the refrigerator, below 4°C/39°F. They should be covered or closely wrapped to protect them from light and air. Keep them away from strong-smelling foods as they can absorb other flavours easily. (The butter storage compartment in most refrigerators is in the door, and is not quite so cold as other parts, so the butter should not become too hard.) Oils tend to solidify at low temperatures, so these are best kept in a cool store cupboard (pantry) at a temperature of 4–12°C/39–54°F, but keep them away from light, which will cause them to deteriorate more quickly.

Above: Margarine tub (left) and block

Right: Very low-fat (left) and low-fat spreads

OILS

These are fats that are liquid at room temperature, and are used in emulsion sauces such as mayonnaise or in salad dressings, usually balanced with vinegar or other acids such as citrus juices. However, they can also be used as a direct replacement for butter or hard fats in roux or other flour-thickened sauces, with good results. With the exception of coconut oil and palm oil, they are mostly rich in unsaturated fat, which helps reduce cholesterol levels. The choice of individual oils for a particular sauce depends largely on flavour and personal taste.

Groundnut (peanut) oil: Made from peanuts, this is usually used where a mild flavour is required.

Sesame seed oil: Usually used for flavouring Asian sauces at the end of cooking, as it has an intense, rich flavour and burns easily when heated. However it can be heated with care, or mixed half and half with another oil, such as groundnut, if necessary.

Soya oil: A mild flavoured oil which will withstand high temperatures. It keeps well and is economical to use.

Sunflower oil: A little more expensive to use than soya oil, this versatile, light-flavoured oil is good for sauces or dressings, as it does not mask other flavours.

Nut oils: Walnut and hazelnut oils are the most commonly used nut oils for dressings, lending their rich, distinctive flavours to salads. Use in moderation, perhaps combined with a milder oil, as the flavours can be strong.

OLIVE OILS

The characteristics and quality of olive oils vary and depend on variety, growing region and method of production. Many are blended, but the best quality oils are produced on individual estates. For most sauces, including mayonnaise, it's best to choose virgin or pure olive oil, and keep the more expensive extra virgin ones for salad dressings, or for drizzling directly over foods. It is more economical to buy olive oils in larger quantities.

Extra virgin first pressed or cold pressed olive oils: These oils are made from what is literally the first pressing of the olives, with no additional treatment such as heat or blending. By law, these oils never have more than 1 per cent acidity, ensuring a fine flavour. They have a very distinctive flavour, as well as a pungent aroma. They are usually a deep green colour and are sometimes cloudy, although both of these factors vary according to the area where the oil has been produced.

Virgin olive oil: This is also cold pressed and unrefined, but has a higher acidity content than extra virgin oil, with a maximum level of 1 to 1.5 per cent.

Pure olive oil: This comes from the third or fourth pressing of the olives, and is usually blended. It has a maximum acid content of 2 per cent. It is widely used in cooking since it is not overpowering.

Light olive oil: This is from the last pressing of the fruit and has the lightest flavour of all.

Below, from left: Groundnut (peanut) oil, sunflower oil, soya oil, sesame oil, walnut oil

The Pantry

A well-stocked pantry makes every cook's life a lot easier, and when it comes to sauce making, it really makes sense. Just by keeping a few basic ingredients in stock, you will always be able to whip up an impromptu sauce when the occasion demands, transforming a simple dish into something really special.

STOCK CUBES AND POWDERS

There is a wide choice of commercial stock (bouillon) cubes and powders on the market, and these vary in flavour and quality. Good-quality products make adequate substitutes for fresh stock, and certainly they are very convenient to use. However, some tend to be quite salty, so allow for this when adding other seasonings. Follow the pack directions for quantities to use. Generally speaking, it is worth paying a little more for good-quality stock cubes or powder, and it is worth choosing one that is made with natural ingredients, which should impart a more natural flavour.

Many supermarkets also now sell ready-made cartons of basic fresh stocks on the chilled foods counter, such as beef, chicken, fish and vegetable stock, and these are a good substitute for home-made if you're short of time to make your own.

Canned consommé makes an excellent substitute for a good brown stock in rich savoury sauces, so is well worth keeping handy in the store cupboard. If you need a light stock, the colour of consommé may be too dark, but brands vary.

CANNED TOMATOES AND SAUCES

Since many of the plum tomatoes we buy out of season in this country are lacking in flavour, it's a safer bet to go for good-quality canned tomatoes in recipes, either whole or chopped. The best are from Italy, so check the label carefully. *Polpa di pomodoro* are finely chopped or crushed.

Avoid those with added herbs or spices, which are best added fresh.

Above: Consommé
Left: Stock (bouillon) cubes and powder
Below, clockwise from left: Passata (bottled strained tomatoes), sugocasa, whole plum tomatoes, tomato purée (paste), chopped tomatoes

Crushed or creamed tomatoes:
Sold as sugocasa, polpa and passata
(bottled strained tomatoes), and usually
packed in convenient jars or bottles,
these are invaluable for sauces. Sugocasa
and polpa have a chunky texture, and
passata is sieved to a smooth purée.

Tomato purée (paste): Concentrated,
cooked tomato pulp in a strong, thick
paste is sold in tubes or cans. The
strength of different brands varies, so use
with care or the flavour can overpower a
sauce. Sun-dried tomato paste is a purée
of sun-dried tomatoes with olive oil. It
has a sweet, rich flavour, and is milder
than ordinary tomato purée.

*Below, top row from left: Oyster sauce, soy
sauce, Worcestershire sauce, fish sauce, hot
pepper sauce. Bottom row: Red pesto, green
pesto, English (hot) mustard*

COOK'S TIP

*Chopped canned tomatoes are usually
more expensive than whole ones, so you
can save housekeeping money by simply
chopping them yourself.*

COMMERCIAL SAUCES

The huge range of commercially-made
flavouring sauces now available is a
boon to the creative cook. Some of
the most useful ones to keep in your
store cupboard (pantry) are:

Hot pepper sauces: Widely used in
West Indian and South American
cooking, there are many versions of
pepper sauce, the most famous being
Tabasco. Use with caution, as they can be
fiery hot. These sauces will pep up the
flavour of almost any savoury sauce,
marinade or dressing.

Mustards: Ready-made mustards are a
blend of ground mustard seeds with flour

and salt, often with wine, herbs and other
spices. Dijon is often used for classic
French sauces and for dressings such as
vinaigrette and mayonnaise – it also helps
to stabilize the emulsion. Yellow English
(hot) mustard is a good choice to give
colour and bite to cheese sauce or to
flavour rich gravies for meat. Milder
German mustard is good for a barbecue
sauce to serve with chops or sausages.
Mild, creamy American mustard is
squeezed on hotdogs or burgers.
Wholegrain mustard gives a pleasant
texture, particularly to creamy savoury
sauces and dressings.

Oyster sauce: A thicker-textured sauce
made with the extract of real oysters,
this adds a delicious sweet-savoury
flavour to sauces for accompanying meat,
fish or vegetables.

Pesto: Commercially made pesto is sold
in jars, either the traditional green basil
pesto, or a red pesto made from sun-
dried tomatoes. Use it
just as it is as a replacement for fresh pesto
sauce to stir into pasta,
pepped up with a little
freshly grated Parmesan
cheese or an extra drizzle
of olive oil. You can
also add it by the
spoonful to enrich

Coconut Milk and Cream

Coconut milk and cream are used widely in Asian dishes, particularly those based on spicy and curried sauces. They can be used rather like dairy products, for thickening, enriching and flavouring.

Coconut milk: This is available in cans and longlife packs. It is similar in thickness to single (light) cream.

Coconut cream: This has the thickness of double (heavy) cream. Creamed coconut (US coconut cream) is solid and white; it is sold in solid blocks, so you can cut off just the amount you need and melt it into sauces.

Right, clockwise from left: Coconut cream, coconut milk, creamed coconut

and enhance the flavour of tomato sauces, salsas and dressings. Once the jar is opened, it should be treated as fresh and stored in the refrigerator.

Soy sauce: Although this is traditionally used for Chinese and Japanese foods, there is no need to limit its use to Asian dishes. Use it to flavour and colour all kinds of savoury sauces, marinades and dressings. Light soy sauce is good in light, sweet-and-sour or stir-fry sauces for fish or vegetables, and the richer, sweeter dark soy sauce is best with rich meat sauces such as satays, or for barbecue sauces.

Thai fish sauce (*nam pla*): This is a classic Thai sauce made from fermented fish. It has a pungent flavour and is best in cooked sauces. It adds a richness to sauces for both meat and fish.

Worcestershire sauce: This classic English sauce has its origins in India. Its spicy, mellowed flavour enhances savoury sauces, marinades and dressings of any type.

VINEGARS

These are made from alcoholic bases of malt, wine, beer, cider (hard cider), rice wine and sugar, and most of these can be used to enhance flavour in sauces

or as emulsifiers. Wine and fruit vinegars are particularly useful for salad dressings, and rice vinegars add authentic flavours to Asian sauces. When using some of the dark, long-matured sherry or balsamic vinegars, bear in mind that they often

have intense, powerful flavours and you may need only a few drops.

Below, from left: Balsamic vinegar, white wine vinegar, red wine vinegar, raspberry vinegar

Herbs and Spices

Many sauce recipes call for herbs and spices to add flavour and colour, and there's no end to the variety you can buy nowadays, especially in the larger supermarkets and good Asian grocers. Generally speaking, herbs are the leafy tops and stems of an edible plant, and spices are from the berries, seeds, bark, and roots.

CULINARY HERBS

It's worth growing a few of the more useful common herbs yourself. Some herbs grown in pots on the kitchen windowsill, will always be handy when you need a few sprigs. It is considerably cheaper, too, as supermarket fresh herbs, even the ones in pots, have a limited life and can be quite costly. A useful basic selection to grow at home would include parsley, chives, thyme, mint, oregano, sage, bay and dill.

When cooking with herbs, you don't need to be too precise. Treat the measurements quoted in recipes as a general guide, and add the herbs according to your personal preference.

DRIED AND FROZEN HERBS

Dried herbs are useful to keep in the pantry for emergencies, but always plump for fresh in preference if you can get them. Many of the delicate-leaved herbs, such as basil or coriander (cilantro), do not dry successfully, but the ones that are

worth buying dried are thyme, rosemary, parsley, mint, oregano, tarragon and dill. Store dried herbs in airtight containers in a cool place away from light, and use them quickly as their flavour is soon lost.

Frozen herbs, such as parsley, chives and coriander, retain more of the flavour of fresh herbs and can be very useful and convenient – they can be added to a sauce or dressing straight from the freezer.

Above, clockwise from top left: Chopped and frozen herbs – coriander (cilantro), parsley, chives

SALT AND PEPPER

Good-quality sea salt has a more intense flavour than "table" or "cooking" salt. Strong black peppercorns, mild white and very mild green are all worth storing.

Below, clockwise from bowl: Tandoori curry paste, nutmeg, cinnamon sticks, vanilla pods (beans), sea salt, whole coriander, cumin seeds, black, green, white peppercorns

Above, clockwise from left: Mint, bay, thyme

Above, clockwise from top: Freeze-dried mint, freeze-dried parsley, freeze-dried dill, freeze-dried tarragon, dried thyme, dried rosemary. Centre: Freeze-dried oregano

SPICES

Keep a good store of spices in the kitchen. A useful selection includes whole nutmeg, cinnamon sticks, vanilla pods (beans), coriander seeds, cumin seeds and curry paste (curry pastes keep for much longer than powders).

Cinnamon sticks: These have a sweet, spicy flavour and are widely used in sweet sauces and chutneys. They can either be crushed or used whole and removed at the end of cooking.

Coriander: These seeds are used in chutneys and have a mild sweet flavour.

Cumin: A key ingredient in chutneys and curries, these seeds have a slightly bitter and strong taste.

Curry paste: This is sold in a range of strengths and flavours. It keeps for much longer than curry powder.

Vanilla pods: Infuse (steep) these dried pods in milk or cream for sweet sauces and custards. Store in a jar of caster (superfine) sugar to make vanilla sugar.

Whole nutmeg: Freshly grated whole nutmeg is much better than the powdered variety, which quickly loses its flavour.

STORING SPICES

Whole spices will store for much longer than ready-ground ones and have a stronger, more intense flavour. Once ground, they begin to lose the volatile oils that give them flavour, so it is best to grind whole spices yourself, either in a pestle and mortar or with a spice mill or using an electric coffee grinder. Buy them little and often and store in airtight containers in a cool, dark, dry store cupboard (pantry). Discard any that have not been used after a year.

Essences and Flower Waters

Vanilla or other essences (extracts) can be very convenient, but choose carefully, as some are inferior artificial flavourings. Check the label – it should describe the contents as pure vanilla essence or extract of vanilla, not vanilla flavouring.

Flower waters are a delightful way to flavour cold sweet sauces, syrups and creams in particular, but occasionally they are used in Middle Eastern savoury sauces. The best known are rose and orange flower water, and should be used in small amounts – the best quality flower waters are triple-distilled, so just a few drops will add a delicately exotic scent to a creamy sauce.

Right, from left: Flower essences (extracts) vanilla essence, almond essence

Dairy Products

The number of sauces based on dairy products is vast, so it is worth taking the time to understand the different products available. You may be aiming for a rich and creamy sauce, or perhaps you would prefer a lighter, healthier alternative. The following descriptions should help.

MILK

The choice of milk for sauces depends upon the richness desired – for a rich flavour and creamy texture, choose whole milk or Channel Islands milk, but if you're watching fat levels and looking for a lighter sauce, it is best to go for skimmed or semi-skimmed (low-fat).

Pasteurized: Most milk sold these days has been pasteurized, i.e. heat-treated, to destroy harmful bacteria. It should keep for up to five days under refrigeration.

Homogenized: This has been processed to distribute the fat globules evenly throughout the milk, instead of rising to the surface as cream. It has the same keeping quality as ordinary milk.

Sterilized: This is homogenized, bottled and then heat-treated for 20 minutes, so that it keeps without refrigeration until it is opened.

UHT: This is homogenized then heat-treated to high temperatures for just one or two seconds. It has a slightly caramelized flavour, but is useful to store as a standby as it keeps unopened for about a year without refrigeration.

Condensed: This sweetened milk is available in cans, and has been boiled to reduce and concentrate it. It is very rich and sweet, but useful for rich dessert sauces. Lower-fat versions are available.

Evaporated: Unsweetened milk that has had some of the water removed by evaporation, this milk has a concentrated flavour and is slightly caramelized. There are also lighter-fat versions available. It is available either in cans or longlife packs.

Goat's milk: Many people who are allergic to cow's milk can tolerate goat's milk, which is now widely available and can be used as a direct substitute for ordinary milk in cooking. It has a similar flavour, although it is slightly sharper, and is more digestible.

CREAM

All kinds of creams can be used to enrich and thicken both sweet and savoury sauces, both hot and cold. The main ones are as follows:

Single (light) cream: This cream has a fat content of just 18 per cent, which is too low for whipping. It will not withstand boiling without splitting, but can be stirred into sauces at the end of cooking to enrich the flavour.

Sour cream: In fact, this is really single cream with an added souring culture, which sharpens the flavour and thickens the texture.

Double (heavy) cream: The fat content of double cream is 48 per cent. The cream almost doubles in bulk when whipped. It is especially good in hot sauces, because it can withstand boiling without separating.

Whipping cream: This has 35 per cent fat, and whips up to a light texture, or can be stirred into sauces after cooking.

Fat Levels in Milk

- Channel Islands (or breakfast milk): 5–8 per cent fat
- Whole milk: 4 per cent fat
- Semi-skimmed: 1.7 per cent fat
- Skimmed: 0.1 per cent fat

COOK'S TIP

When whipping double cream, you can reduce the risk of overbeating and extend the volume by adding 15ml/1 tbsp milk to each 150ml/¼ pint/⅔ cup cream. Use a hand whisk instead of an electric one, so you have more control over the speed.

CRÈME FRAÎCHE

This has a mild, tangy flavour similar to that of sour cream, which makes it great for using in both sweet and savoury sauces

Below, from left: Skimmed milk, semi-skimmed (low-fat) milk, whole milk, Channel Islands milk, evaporated milk, condensed milk

and dressings. With a fat content of around 40 per cent, it is more stable than sour cream when heated. You can also buy a half-fat version, which can be successfully added to hot sauces without curdling.

YOGURT

Yogurt and other lower-fat dairy products make excellent lighter replacements for cream in many sweet and savoury sauces, and can be used as a direct substitute to add a lighter tang to all kinds of uncooked sauces. For cooked sauces, yogurt should be stabilized first with cornflour (cornstarch).

Greek (US strained plain) yogurt: This may be made from either cow's or sheep's milk. It is richer in flavour and texture than most yogurts, but still only has a fat content of around 8–10 per cent, so it makes a light substitute for cream in sauces.

Low-fat yogurt: It is the use of semi-skimmed (low-fat) milk that makes this yogurt low-fat. Very low-fat yogurt is made with skimmed milk. Both types have quite a sharp, tangy flavour which can be refreshing in light sauces and dips.

Above, clockwise from left: Single (light) cream, double (heavy) cream, crème fraîche, sour cream, whipping cream

Above: Greek (US strained plain) yogurt (left), low-fat yogurt

STABILIZING YOGURT FOR SAUCES

To prevent yogurt splitting in cooked sauces, allow 5ml/1 tsp cornflour to each 150ml/ ¼ pint/⅔ cup yogurt. Blend the cornflour and a little yogurt to a smooth paste before adding the rest of the yogurt. Add to the sauce and cook as instructed in the recipe.

Above: Eggs

EGGS

As a general rule, medium (US large) eggs are the size to use for recipes, unless stated otherwise, but you may find it useful to have small (US medium) eggs for using to enrich or thicken sauces.

The freshness of eggs is easier to ensure nowadays, as most are now individually marked with a date stamp on their shells. Fresh eggs should store well for two weeks, providing that the shell is not damaged or dirty. Egg shells are porous, so they are best stored at the bottom of the refrigerator away from strong smelling foods. Before use, eggs should be left at room temperature for about 30 minutes.

SAFETY TIP

Because of the slight risk of contamination in raw eggs, it is recommended that pregnant women, young children, elderly people or anyone weakened by chronic illness should avoid eating raw or lightly cooked eggs.

CHEESE

Many hard cheeses can be grated and melted into sauces. Strong, hard cheeses such as mature (sharp) Cheddar, Gruyère and Parmesan will grate easily and melt into hot sauces. Their fine flavour complements pasta sauces or a creamy white sauce to pour over vegetables. Always grate these cheeses freshly as you need them, and never use ready-grated Parmesan, as the flavour is soon lost after grating. Once you've added cheese to a sauce, heat it gently without boiling, or the cheese will overcook and become stringy.

Soft, fresh cheeses such as ricotta or mascarpone are also used to enrich a wide range of sauces and dips, from tomato sauces to fruit purées or custards. Ricotta is light in texture and mild in flavour, and makes a good base for dips instead of yogurt, or can be melted into hot sauces. Mascarpone has a luxuriously rich texture, creamy and high in fat, and can be used in the same way as thick cream.

Below, clockwise from top: Parmesan, mascarpone, ricotta, Cheddar, Gruyère

Sauce-making Equipment

Making sauces requires very little in the way of specialist equipment, but a carefully selected set of basic equipment will help make tasks such as boiling, whisking and straining much easier. You may even find that most of these items are already in your kitchen. Shop around for those you still need, as quality varies enormously.

PANS

The rule here is to choose the right pan for the job, which means that your pans do not necessarily have to be a matching set. Some pans may be suitable for more than one task, but you will need a variety of sizes and types. Look for solid, heavy pans that are stable when empty, and have tight-fitting lids and firmly riveted handles. Buying good-quality pans is an investment, as they will last for years. Cheap, thin pans will not only wear out quickly, they will also conduct heat unevenly and cause burnt spots. A good selection would be:

• Milk pan with high sides and a lip. This may be non-stick, but is not essential.

• Three pans with lids, ranging in size from about 1 litre/1¾ pints/4 cups to 7 litres/12⅓ pints/30 cups. They should be deep and straight-sided to minimize evaporation.

• Sauté pan with deep, straight sides.

• Double boiler – a useful pan for making delicate creams and custards, and melting ingredients such as chocolate. If you don't have one, improvise with a heatproof bowl placed over a pan of hot water.

MATERIALS FOR PANS

Stainless steel: Attractive and hard-wearing, and providing they have a thick base with aluminium (aluminum) or copper, the pans will conduct heat evenly and well.

Anodized aluminium: Light and easy to clean, this conducts the heat well and does not corrode. The metal reacts when in contact with acid and alkaline, so food should not be left to stand for too long in these pans.

Copper: These pans are expensive but conduct heat very efficiently and

*Top: Double boiler and heatproof bowl placed over pan
Right, from left: Enamelled, anodized aluminium (aluminum) and copper pans*

Above, from left: Spiral sauce whisks, balloon whisk, wooden spoons

are attractive and durable. Choose pans with a stainless steel lining, which is harder-wearing than tin.

Enamelled cast iron: This is heavy, but conducts the heat well, evenly and slowly. These pans retain the heat for a long time, and are hard-wearing and durable.

WOODEN SPOONS

A good assortment of wooden spoons is essential, and it is a good idea to keep them for individual uses. For example, you might reserve one for spicy sauces, one for creams and custards, and so on; then there is no risk of flavour transfer. A good selection includes a wooden spoon, a wooden corner spoon with an edge to reach into the corners of pans, and a flat-edged wooden spatula, for efficient stirring without scratching.

WHISKS

Balloon whisks and spiral sauce whisks are the most efficient for blending sauce ingredients or whisking dressings, and it is useful to have two different sizes. Choose ones with a comfortable grip.

LADLES

Available in various sizes, ladles are very useful for spooning and pouring sauces over foods. Some smaller ones have a useful lip for more precise pouring. Stainless steel ladles are the best. A slotted stainless steel draining spoon is invaluable for skimming and removing small pieces of ingredients from sauces.

Bottom, from left: Slotted spoon, ladles

MEASURING JUG (CUP)

Choose a solid jug marked clearly with standard measurements. Heatproof glass is ideal, as it is easy to see the liquid level and can take boiling liquids, yet the handle remains cool as it is a poor conductor of heat. Stainless steel jugs are attractive and hard-wearing.

MEASURING SPOONS

A set of British Standard measuring spoons marked in imperial and metric, is essential for accurate measuring of small

Below, from top: Hand-held electric whisk, hand blender
Right, from top: Sieve and chinois, measuring jug and spoons

amounts of sauce ingredients, as ordinary kitchen spoons vary in capacity. Spoon measurements given in recipes are always level.

SIEVE AND CHINOIS

A fine-meshed stainless steel sieve is essential for sauce making, and it can also be very useful to have a chinois, a cone-shaped sieve that is used for straining and puréeing a range of ingredients.

ELECTRICAL EQUIPMENT

Although not essential for making sauces, a blender, food processor, hand blender or whisk can take much of the hard work out of many sauces and dressings.

Hand-held electric blenders are perhaps more versatile and convenient than larger machines for sauces, as they can be used to blend or purée ingredients directly in a pan or jug (pitcher), and are easy to clean by simply swishing in hot soapy water after use. A hand-held electric whisk is also invaluable for quick and easy beating and whisking.

Making Basic Stocks

A good home-made stock is simple to make and adds a rich flavour to all kinds of savoury sauces. Commercial stock (bouillon) cubes and bouillon powder won't match the flavour of home-made stock. However, they can be very useful for enriching a stock that lacks flavour: heat it until boiling then stir in a stock cube or a teaspoon of bouillon powder until dissolved. Each recipe below makes approximately 1 litre/1¾ pints/4 cups.

Beef Stock

INGREDIENTS

675g/1½lb shin of beef, diced
1 large onion, chopped
1 large carrot, chopped
1 celery stick, chopped
bouquet garni
6 black peppercorns
2.5ml/½ tsp sea salt
1.75 litres/3 pints/7½ cups water

1 Place all the ingredients in a large pan and gradually bring to the boil.

2 Cover the pan and simmer very gently for 4 hours, skimming occasionally to remove scum. Strain the stock and cool.

Fish Stock

INGREDIENTS

1kg/2¼lb white fish bones and trimmings
1 large onion, sliced
1 large carrot, sliced
1 celery stick, sliced
bouquet garni
6 white peppercorns
2.5ml/½ tsp sea salt
150ml/¼ pint/⅔ cup dry white wine
1 litre/1¾ pints/4 cups water

1 Place the ingredients in a pan and bring to the boil.

2 Skim any scum from the surface, cover the pan and simmer for 20 minutes. Strain and cool.

Chicken Stock

INGREDIENTS

1 chicken carcass
chicken giblets
1 leek, chopped
1 celery stick, chopped
bouquet garni
5ml/1 tsp white peppercorns
2.5ml/½ tsp sea salt
1.75 litres/3 pints/7½ cups water

1 Break up the carcass, place in a pan with the remaining ingredients. Bring to the boil.

2 Reduce the heat, cover and simmer gently for about 2½ hours, skimming to remove scum. Strain the stock and cool.

Vegetable Stock

INGREDIENTS

500g/1¼lb chopped mixed vegetables, e.g. onions, carrots, celery, leeks
bouquet garni
6 black peppercorns
2.5ml/½ tsp sea salt
1 litre/1¾ pints/4 cups water

1 Place all the ingredients in a large pan and slowly bring to the boil.

2 Skim any scum from the surface, then cover the pan and simmer gently for 30 minutes. Strain the stock and allow to cool.

Making a Bouquet Garni

A traditional bouquet garni usually contains a bay leaf, a sprig of thyme and a few sprigs of parsley, but this can be varied according to taste, and to suit the dish you are making. Other vegetables or herbs you may like to include are a piece of celery stick for poultry dishes; a rosemary sprig for beef or lamb; or a piece of fennel or leek, or a strip of lemon rind, to flavour fish dishes.

Tie the herbs together firmly with fine cotton string, so the bundle is easy to remove from the stock after cooking.

Or, tie the herbs in a square of muslin (cheesecloth). Leave a long length of the string to tie to the pan handle.

Keeping Stock Clear

For a clear soup it is important to keep the stock clear; avoid boiling the soup, and skim the top from time to time.

1 Trim any fat from the meat or bones before adding to the stock pan, as this can create a cloudy stock.

2 Keep the heat at a low simmer, and skim off any scum as it gathers on the surface during cooking. Most vegetables can be added to stock for flavour, but potatoes tend to break down and make the stock cloudy so it's best to avoid these.

3 Strain the cooked stock through a sieve lined with muslin (cheese-cloth), and avoid pressing the solids, as this may spoil the stock's clarity.

Removing Fat from Stock

Excess fat should always be removed from the liquid to improve the look and taste of the stock; it also helps keep the stock clear.

1 Let the stock stand until the fat settles on the surface, then skim off as much fat as possible with a large, shallow spoon. To absorb even more grease, blot the surface of the stock with several layers of kitchen paper.

2 Then, drop in a few ice cubes. The fat will set around the ice so it can be simply spooned off.

3 Alternatively, allow the stock to cool on a work surface, then chill in the refrigerator until the fat layer rises to the surface and sets. Then the fat can simply be lifted off. Use a large spoon to remove the solidified fat and discard it.

How to Store Stock

Stock will keep for up to a week in the refrigerator, and freezes well. Reduce it first so that it takes up less room in the freezer.

1 To freeze, pour into airtight containers, allowing 2.5cm/1in headspace for expansion, then seal and freeze for up to 3 months.

2 To freeze stock in convenient portions to add to sauces, pour into ice cube trays for freezing.

COOK'S TIP

• *Use salt sparingly at the beginning of cooking – if you are going to reduce the stock it will become much more salty.*
• *To make a brown stock from beef or veal bones, roast the bones in a hot oven for 40 minutes. Add the vegetables half-way through the roasting time. Deglaze the pan with a little water and simmer the bones and vegetables as usual.*
• *To make a stock with a concentrated flavour, simmer the stock until reduced by half. Continue to reduce the stock until it will coat the back of a spoon. At its most concentrated it will set as a solid jelly and give you a quick and easy way to add rich flavour to sauces and soups.*

Flour-based Sauces

Flour-based Sauces

The standard way to adjust the consistency of a sauce is to thicken it with one of the different available types of flour. There are three basic methods for this – roux, blending or all-in-one. Once you've learned the basic skills of these methods, you'll be able to tackle any flour-thickened sauce without problems.

Many of the classic white sauces are based on a "roux", which is simply a cooked mixture of flour and fat. The most basic white sauce uses milk, but by varying the liquid used other well-known white sauces can be made. For a classic béchamel sauce, the milk is flavoured first by infusing (steeping) with pieces of vegetables and herbs. For velouté sauce, the milk is replaced with stock, giving the sauce a more opaque appearance, and the thickened sauce may be enriched with cream after cooking. Brown sauces or gravy are made by browning the roux, usually with onions, before adding stock or other liquid such as wine.

Basic Recipe for White Roux Sauces

Using the classic roux method, you can adjust the amount of thickening to create varying consistencies of sauces. A pouring sauce is used, as it suggests, to be poured directly over foods when serving. The slightly thicker coating sauce is used to make a smooth covering for fish or vegetables.

For a pouring consistency:
15g/¹/₂ oz/1 tbsp butter
15g/¹/₂ oz/2 tbsp flour
300ml/¹/₂ pint/1¼ cups liquid

For a coating consistency:
25g/1 oz/2 tbsp butter
25g/1 oz/¼ cup flour
300 ml/¹/₂ pint/1¼ cups liquid

Making a Roux-based White Sauce

The trick to making a roux is to stir the pan over the whole of the base, and add the liquid gradually; it is a good idea to heat the milk or stock before adding to the roux as this helps avoid lumps.

Melt the butter in a pan, then add the flour. To prevent browning, cook on a low heat and stir with a wooden spoon, for 1–2 minutes. Allow the mixture to bubble until it resembles a honeycomb in texture. It is important to cook well at this point, to allow the starch grains in the flour to swell and burst, and avoid lumps forming later.

2 Remove the pan from the heat and gradually stir in the liquid, which may be either hot or cold. Return to the heat and stir until boiling and thickened. Reduce the heat and simmer, stirring constantly, for 2 minutes, until the sauce is thickened and smooth.

Blending Method

Sauces which are thickened by the blending method are usually made with cornflour (cornstarch), arrowroot, potato flour or sauce flour. Cornflour and sauce flour make light, glossy, lump-free sauces, which are good for freezing as the starch does not break down. If you need a crystal-clear result for glazing, use arrowroot or potato flour. The liquid may be milk, stock, fruit juice, or syrup from canned or poached fruit. As a guide, you will need 20g/¾ oz/3 tbsp cornflour or sauce flour to thicken 300ml/¹/₂ pint/1¼ cups liquid to a pouring consistency. Arrowroot or potato flour are slightly stronger, so use approximately 15g/¹/₂ oz to 300ml/¹/₂ pint/1¼ cups liquid to obtain the same consistency.

Place the flour in a bowl and add just enough liquid to make a smooth, thin paste. Heat the remaining liquid in a pan until almost boiling.

2 Pour a little of the liquid on to the blended mixture, stirring. Pour the blended mixture back into the pan, whisking constantly to avoid lumps. Return to the heat and stir until boiling, then simmer gently for 2 minutes, stirring until thickened and smooth.

All-in-one Method

This method uses the same ingredients and proportions as the roux method, but the liquid added must be cold.

Place the flour, butter and cold liquid in the pan and whisk with a sauce whisk or balloon whisk over a moderate heat until boiling. Stir over the heat for 2 minutes, until thickened and smooth.

Using an Egg Yolk Liaison

This is a simple way to lightly thicken hot milk or stock, cream or reduced poaching liquids, and is good for enriching savoury white or velouté sauces. Two egg yolks should be enough to enrich and thicken about 300ml/½ pint/1¼ cups liquid, depending on the recipe. A mixture of egg yolk and cream has the same effect, but add it when the pan is off the heat to avoid curdling.

Place two egg yolks in a small bowl and stir in 30ml/2 tbsp of the hot liquid or sauce. Stir the egg mixture into the remaining liquid or sauce and heat gently, stirring, without boiling.

Making Beurre Manié

Literally translated as "kneaded butter", this is a mixture of flour and butter, which can be stirred into a hot sauce, poaching liquid or cooked dish such as a casserole or ragoût to thicken the juices. It's a convenient way to adjust the consistency of a sauce or dish at the end of cooking, and is easy to control as you can add the exact amount required, adjusting as it thickens. The butter adds flavour and a glossy sheen to the finished sauce. Any leftover beurre manié can be stored in a covered jar in the refrigerator for about 2 weeks, ready to use in sauces, soups, stews or casseroles.

Place equal amounts of butter and flour in a bowl and knead together with your fingers or a wooden spoon to make a smooth paste.

2 Drop teaspoonfuls of the beurre manié paste into the simmering sauce, whisking thoroughly to incorporate each spoonful before adding the next, until the sauce is thickened and smooth and the desired consistency is achieved.

Infusing Flavours

To infuse (steep) flavours into milk, stock or other liquids before using in sauces such as béchamel, pour the liquid into a pan and add thin slices or dice of onion, carrot and celery, a bouquet garni, peppercorns or a mace blade. Bring the liquid slowly to the boil, then remove the pan from the heat. Cover and leave to stand for about 10 minutes. Strain the milk to remove the flavourings before use.

Adding Flavourings to Flour-based Sauces

Once you've made your basic sauce, try some of these quick flavour additions to pep up the flavour and add variety:
• Stir 50g/2oz/½ cup grated Cheddar or other strong cheese into a basic white sauce with 5ml/1 tsp wholegrain mustard and a generous dash of Worcestershire sauce.
• Wine livens up the flavour of most stock-based sauces – boil 60ml/4 tbsp red or white wine in a pan until wellreduced, then stir into the finished sauce with a grating of nutmeg or black pepper.
• Parsley, or any fresh herbs will infuse and change the flavour of a white sauce. Add chopped herbs a few minutes before the end of the cooking time.

Correcting a Lumpy Sauce

If your flour-thickened sauce has gone lumpy, don't despair – it can be corrected.

| First, try whisking the sauce hard with a light wire whisk in the pan to smooth out the lumps, then reheat gently, stirring.

2 If the sauce is still not smooth, rub it through a fine sieve, pressing firmly with a wooden spoon. Return to the pan and reheat gently, stirring.

3 Alternatively, pour the sauce into a food processor and process until smooth. Return to the pan and reheat gently, stirring.

Keeping Sauces Hot

| To keep sauces hot, pour into a heatproof bowl and place over a pan of very gently simmering water.

2 To prevent a skin from forming over the surface, place a sheet of lightly oiled or wetted greaseproof (waxed) paper or baking parchment directly on to the surface of the sauce. Stir before serving.

Degreasing Sauces

Even after skimming any surplus fat from a finished hot sauce or gravy with a flat metal spoon, final traces of fat may still remain. These can be removed by dragging the flat surface of a piece of kitchen paper over the surface to absorb traces of grease.

Making a Roux-based Brown Sauce

A brown roux is the basis of many meat dish sauces. Onions or other vegetables are usually browned in fat before flour is added. The fat can be a mixture of butter and oil, or dripping. Butter alone is unsuitable as it burns easily at high temperatures. Use about 30ml/2 tbsp oil and about 25g/1oz/¼ cup flour for the roux to about 600ml/1 pint/2½ cups reduced brown stock. At the last moment, stir in 15g/½oz/1 tbsp chilled butter to give a glossy finish.

| Melt the fat and fry one small, finely chopped onion until softened and golden. Sprinkle on the flour and stir in with a wooden spoon. Stir over a low heat for 4–5 minutes, until the mixture colours to a rich brown.

2 Remove the pan from the heat and gradually stir in the liquid, which may be either hot or cold. Return to the heat and stir until boiling. Simmer gently, stirring, for a further 2 minutes, until the sauce is thick and smooth. The sauce may be strained to remove the onions at this stage.

Using a Deglazed Sauce

Deglazing means adding a small amount of liquid to the pan after roasting or pan-frying to dilute the rich concentrated juices into a simple sauce. Spoon off the excess fat, and then scrape up the sediment from the pan bottom with a spoon as you stir in the liquid.

1 Tilt the pan and spoon off excess fat from the surface of the juices.

2 Stir in a few tablespoons of wine, stock or cream.

3 Simmer over a moderate heat, stirring and scraping up the sediment as the sauce boils. Boil rapidly to reduce the juices until syrupy, then pour over the food.

Making Traditional Gravy

Good gravy should be smooth and glossy, never heavy and floury. Generally speaking, it's best to use the minimum of thickening, but this can be adjusted to your own taste. Providing the meat has been roasted to a rich brown, the meat juices will have enough colour to colour the gravy. If it is too pale, a few drops of gravy browning can be stirred in to darken it slightly.

1 To make a thickened gravy, skim off all except about 15ml/1 tbsp of the fat from the juices in the roasting pan after roasting meat. Gradually stir in about 15ml/1 tbsp flour, scraping up the sediment and meat juices.

2 Place the tin directly over the heat and stir until bubbling. Cook, stirring for 1–2 minutes until the roux is brown and the flour cooked.

3 Gradually stir in the liquid, which may be either stock or vegetable water, until the gravy is of the thickness desired. Simmer for 2–3 minutes, stirring constantly, and adjust the seasoning to taste.

Ideas for Deglazed Sauces
Brandy and Peppercorn – deglaze the pan with brandy or sherry, stir in cream and coarsely ground black pepper. Serve with grilled (broiled) or fried steaks.
Red Wine and Cranberry – deglaze the pan with red wine and stir in cranberry sauce or jelly. This recipe is good with roast game or turkey.
Sauce Bercy – deglaze with dry white wine or vermouth, stir in a finely chopped shallot and sauté gently until soft. Add cream, lemon juice and chopped parsley. Excellent with fried or poached fish.

Adding Flavourings to a Brown Sauce
A well-flavoured brown stock, which has been reduced by between one-third to a half, is the basis of a good brown sauce but it can also be enhanced by the addition of a variety of flavourings.
• A handful of chopped fresh basil, chives or flat leaf parsley, stirred into the sauce just before serving, will improve the flavour and look of a basic brown sauce.
• For game or poultry, stir a little curry paste, two crushed cloves of garlic and one finely chopped onion into the roux and cook for about 5 minutes before adding the stock. Stir in a handful of chopped fresh coriander (cilantro) just before serving.
• Add coarsely grated orange rind to a basic brown sauce and serve it with duck or game.

Vegetable Sauces and Salsas

Many sauces use vegetables for flavour, colour and texture, and there's no end to the healthy variations you can make with a few very simple techniques. Puréed or chopped vegetables can be used to make both cooked sauces and fresh salsas. Vegetable sauces and salsas make fresh, colourful, low-fat alternatives to more conventional sauces, and they are invariably very easy and quick to make.

Basic Tomato Sauce

For the best flavour, use plum tomatoes. If using canned make sure they are not already flavoured with herbs. Peel fresh tomatoes before using. Fresh tomatoes rather than canned tomatoes can be used. Substitute about 500g/1¼lb of tomatoes for each 400g/14oz can.

Makes about 450ml/¾ pint/ scant 2 cups

INGREDIENTS

15ml/1 tbsp olive oil
15g/½oz/1 tbsp butter
1 garlic clove, finely chopped
1 small onion, finely chopped
1 celery stick, finely chopped
400g/14oz can chopped tomatoes
handful of basil leaves
salt and ground black pepper

I Heat the olive oil and butter in a heavy pan.

2 When the oil starts to bubble, add the garlic, onion and celery. Sauté the ingredients gently over a low heat, stirring occasionally, for 15–20 minutes or until the onions soften and are just beginning to colour.

3 Stir the chopped tomatoes into the sauce and bring to the boil. Cover and simmer gently for 10–15 minutes, stirring occasionally, until thick.

4 Tear or roughly chop the basil leaves and stir into the sauce. Adjust the seasoning with salt and pepper and serve hot.

COOK'S TIP

A soffritto (Italian), or sofrito (Spanish), is the basis of many Mediterranean meat or tomato sauces. It's such a classic that some recipes list "soffritto" simply as an ingredient with no other explanation. A basic soffritto usually consists of onion, garlic, green (bell) pepper and celery, sometimes with a little carrot or pancetta. The finely chopped ingredients are sautéed slowly to soften and caramelize the flavours and are used in soups and sauces.

Making Quick Salsa Crudo

This is literally a "raw sauce" of vegetables or fruits, and it's easy to create your own combinations of flavour. A good basic start for a salsa crudo is chillies, (bell) peppers, onions, and garlic. Serve with grilled (broiled) chicken, pork, lamb or fish.

I Peel, seed or trim the vegetables as necessary, then use a sharp knife to cut into small, even dice. Try to combine texture and colour as well as taste, and use chillies and other very spicy ingredients sparingly. Put all the diced ingredients into a bowl.

2 Add 15–30ml/1–2 tbsp olive oil and a squeeze of lime or lemon juice and stir in finely chopped fresh basil, coriander (cilantro), flat leaf parsley or mint, to enrich the flavour. Season to taste and toss well before serving.

To Peel Tomatoes

1 Cut a small cross in the skins of the tomatoes. Bring a pan of water to the boil and add the tomatoes. Turn off the heat and leave for 30 seconds, then lift out carefully with a slotted spoon and place in a bowl of cold water. Using a small knife, peel off the skins.

2 Alternatively, place the tomato firmly on the prongs of a fork and hold in a gas flame until the skin blisters and splits. When the tomatoes are cool enough to handle, peel off the skins using a small knife.

Chargrilling Vegetables for Purées and Sauces

Many puréed sauces or salsas call for cooked or chargrilled vegetables. Chargrilling on a barbecue is the best way to get the finest flavour from many vegetables, such as (bell) peppers, aubergines (eggplants), tomatoes, garlic or onions, tenderizing the flesh and retaining and caramelizing the flavourful juices. Since this method is not always practical, the next best is to roast the vegetables under a grill (broiler).

Roasted Vegetable Sauce

Serve roasted vegetable sauce with pork, ham, poultry or game. If you prefer a sauce with more texture, simply process for a shorter time.

Makes about 300ml/¹/₂ pint/1¹/₄ cups

INGREDIENTS

2 red or orange (bell) peppers
1 small onion
1 small aubergine (eggplant)
2 tomatoes with skins removed
2 garlic cloves, unpeeled
30–45ml/2–3 tbsp olive oil
15ml/1 tbsp lemon juice
25g/1oz/¹/₂ cup fresh white breadcrumbs

1 Cut the peppers, onion and aubergine in half, leaving the skins on, and, if necessary, remove any seeds and core. Place the vegetables cut-side down on a baking sheet with the garlic cloves. Place under a very hot grill (broiler) or in a hot oven until the skins are blackened and charred, and the flesh is tender.

2 Remove from the heat and leave until cool enough to handle, then peel off the skins from the peppers and onions.

3 Scoop the flesh from the aubergines, and squeeze the flesh from the garlic.

4 Place all the vegetables in a blender or food processor and process to a very smooth purée, adding oil and lemon juice to taste. If you prefer a very smooth sauce, rub the purée through a fine sieve.

5 To thicken a vegetable purée, stir in a handful of fresh breadcrumbs and process for a few seconds to the desired consistency.

Savoury Butter Sauces

The simplest sauce of all is a melted butter sauce, flavoured with lemon juice or herbs – ideal to drizzle over a simply cooked piece of fish or vegetables. A more refined version of this is clarified butter sauce, which is butter with the moisture and impurities removed. Emulsions of butter with vinegar or other flavourings make deliciously rich beurre blanc or hollandaise sauce. Cold, flavoured butters are useful to add last-minute melting flavours on to hot foods, and can be shaped prettily for extra garnish.

Blender Hollandaise

Hollandaise is a wonderfully rich butter sauce, rather like a hot mayonnaise. This quick method eliminates whisking by hand and uses a blender to incorporate the ingredients to a thick, smooth emulsion where two liquids are combined by the dispersion of one in the other.

Makes 250ml/8fl oz/1 cup

INGREDIENTS

60ml/4 tbsp white wine vinegar
6 peppercorns
1 bay leaf
3 egg yolks
175g/6oz/¾ cup clarified butter
salt and ground black pepper

| Place the wine vinegar, peppercorns and bay leaf in a small pan and heat until boiling, then simmer to reduce to about 15ml/1 tbsp. Remove from the heat and discard the flavourings.

2 Place the egg yolks in the blender goblet and start the motor. Add the reduced white wine vinegar liquid through the feeder tube and blend for 10 seconds.

3 Heat the butter until hot. With the motor running, pour the butter through the feeder tube in a thin, steady stream until thick and smooth. Adjust the seasoning to taste with salt and pepper, and serve warm with poached fish, eggs or vegetables.

PREVENTING CURDLING

If hollandaise sauce is overheated, or if the butter is added too quickly, it may curdle and become slightly granular in texture. If this happens, remove it from the heat immediately, before the sauce separates.

Quickly drop an ice cube into the sauce, then beat hard until the cube melts and cools the sauce. It also helps to stand the base of the pan in a bowl of iced water while whisking in the ice cube.

Beurre Blanc

This is one of the simplest sauces to make. White wine and white wine vinegar are reduced over a high heat to produce an intense flavour. Butter is whisked into the liquid to enrich and thicken it. It is good with grilled (broiled) or poached fish or chicken.

| Place 45ml/3 tbsp each of white wine vinegar and dry white wine in a small pan with a finely chopped shallot. Bring to the boil and boil until reduced to about 15ml/1 tbsp.

2 Cut 225g/8oz/1 cup chilled unsalted (sweet) butter into small cubes. On a low heat, gradually whisk in the butter, piece by piece, allowing each piece to melt and be absorbed before adding the next. Season to taste and serve immediately.

How to Clarify Butter

Ideal for serving with vegetables such as asparagus or artichokes, clarified butter is butter which has been melted and has had all the salts, moisture and impurities removed, leaving it clear, with a rich, pure flavour. Clarified butter, called ghee in Indian cooking, keeps longer and can be heated to higher temperatures than ordinary butter without the risk of burning. It can be used for sautéing, and in sauces it gives a mild flavour and a high gloss. There are two main methods of clarifying:

Place the butter in a pan with an equal quantity of water. Heat until the butter melts. Remove the pan from the heat and leave to cool until the butter sets. Carefully lift out the fat, leaving the water and solids behind.

Alternatively, melt the butter in a small pan over a very low heat, then skim off the froth with a slotted spoon. Pour the rest through a sieve lined with fine muslin (cheesecloth), to strain out the solids.

Making Savoury Butters

Flavoured butters can be shaped or piped decoratively to serve with steaks or poached or grilled (broiled) fish.

To make a herb-flavoured butter, finely chop your choice of fresh herbs. Beat the butter until softened then stir in the herbs to mix evenly.

Making Shaped Slices

To make butter slices, chill the softened herb butter lightly. With your hands, roll the butter into a long sausage-shape and wrap in baking parchment or clear film (plastic wrap). Chill and cut off slices of the butter as required.

Piping Butter

Using a star nozzle, pipe softened butter on to baking parchment.

Making Shaped Butters

To make shaped butter pats, chill lightly, roll out the butter between two sheets of baking parchment. Chill until firm, then remove the top sheet and stamp out small shapes with a cutter.

Flavourings for Savoury Butters

As well as being the traditional accompaniment to steaks, flavoured butters can be rubbed on to meat before roasting or spread over chops before grilling (broiling) or cooking on a barbecue. They can also be spread on fish that is foil-wrapped and baked or used as you would garlic butter to make deliciously flavoured breads.

• Finely chopped herbs, e.g. chives, parsley, dill, mint, thyme or rosemary. Use one herb or a combination of your choice and add as much as the butter will comfortably absorb, or to achieve the desired flavour.
• Finely grated lemon, lime or orange rind and juice.
• Finely chopped canned anchovy fillets.
• Finely chopped gherkins or capers.
• Crushed, dried chillies or finely chopped fresh chillies.
• Crushed, fresh garlic cloves, or roasted garlic purée.
• Ground coriander seeds, curry spices or paste.

Savoury Egg Sauces

The versatility of eggs comes in useful in all kinds of sauces, most commonly for thickening and enriching cooked sauces, or for holding an emulsion such as in mayonnaise. Keep spare egg yolks in the freezer, ready to enrich sauces whenever needed – stir in a pinch of salt or sugar before freezing to prevent them from thickening.

Mayonnaise

The texture of a hand-whisked mayonnaise is quite unlike any other – smooth, glossy and rich, the perfect partner to delicately poached salmon or a chicken salad. The choice of oil for mayonnaise depends on personal taste, but most people would find mayonnaise made with extra virgin olive oil rather too powerful in flavour. So, it's a good idea to use either a pure olive oil, or alternatively use a mix of half pure olive oil with half sunflower oil, or another lighter-flavoured oil.

It is easier to get a good emulsion and prevent the mayonnaise curdling if all the ingredients are at room temperature.

Makes about 300ml/½ pint/1¼ cups

INGREDIENTS

2 egg yolks
15ml/1 tbsp lemon juice
5ml/1 tsp Dijon mustard
300ml/½ pint/1¼ cups light olive oil
salt and ground black pepper

1 Place the egg yolks, lemon juice, mustard, salt and pepper in a bowl and beat the egg yolk mixture until smooth and evenly combined.

2 Pouring with one hand and whisking with the other, add the oil gradually, drop by drop, making sure that each drop is whisked in before adding more.

3 Once a thick emulsion has formed, the oil can be poured faster, in a fine, steady stream, whisking until the mixture becomes smooth and thick. Adjust the seasoning to taste.

Using a Food Processor for Mayonnaise

A food processor can speed up the making of mayonnaise. Use a whole egg instead of the egg yolks.

Process the egg and flavourings for a few seconds then slowly pour in the oil through the feeder tube in a thin, steady stream with the motor running, until the mixture forms a smooth, creamy texture.

Preventing Mayonnaise from Separating

If the oil is added too quickly, the mayonnaise may separate, but this can be corrected if you work quickly.

Break a fresh egg yolk into a clean bowl. Gradually whisk in the separated mayonnaise, a small spoonful at a time, whisking constantly until it begins to thicken. Continue until all the mixture has been incorporated.

MAYONNAISE VARIATIONS

• For Garlic Mayonnaise, add in three to six crushed garlic cloves.
• For Spicy Mayonnaise, add in 15ml/1 tbsp mustard, 7–15ml/ ½–1 tsp Worcestershire sauce and a dash of Tabasco sauce.
• For Green Mayonnaise, combine 25g/1oz each parsley and watercress sprigs in a blender or food processor. Add three or four chopped spring onions (scallions) and one garlic clove. Blend until finely chopped. Add 120ml/4fl oz/½ cup mayonnaise and blend until smooth. Season to taste.
• For Blue Cheese Dressing, mix 225g/8oz crumbled Danish blue cheese into the mayonnaise.

Sweet Egg Sauces

Sweet egg sauces include many rich and creamy techniques, from classic egg-based custards to serve with winter puddings to light and fluffy sabayon which can be served on its own or as a luxurious sauce for gilded fruits, or traditional baked custard which can be served hot or cold.

Egg Custard Sauce

Crème anglaise is the traditional vanilla custard sauce made with eggs, a far cry from the quick custard powder versions so often used. As well as being served as a classic sauce, either hot or cold, *crème anglaise* is often used as the base for other sweet sauces, such as the *crème pâtissière* used to fill éclairs and profiteroles. It's frequently enriched with cream instead of milk, or flavoured with liqueurs for special desserts.

The trick here is to be patient – the egg must be cooked slowly; if it's overheated it will turn to scrambled egg.

Makes about 400ml/14fl oz/1⅔ cups

INGREDIENTS

300ml/½ pint /1¼ cups milk
1 vanilla pod (bean)
3 egg yolks
15ml/1 tbsp caster (superfine) sugar

| Heat the milk with the vanilla pod until just boiling, then remove from the heat. (To intensify the flavour split the pod lengthways.) Cover and leave to infuse (steep) for 10 minutes then strain into a clean pan. Beat the eggs and sugar together lightly in a bowl.

2 Pour the milk on to the eggs, whisking constantly.

3 Pour into the pan and stir until the custard thickens just enough to coat the back of a wooden spoon. Remove from the heat and pour into a jug (pitcher) to prevent overcooking.

Preventing Curdling

Remove the pan from the heat and plunge the base into cold water. Whisk in a teaspoon of cornflour (cornstarch) until smooth, then reheat.

Sabayon Sauce

| Whisk one egg yolk and 15ml/1 tbsp caster (superfine) sugar per portion in a bowl over a pan of simmering water. Whisk in 30ml/2 tbsp sweet white wine, liqueur or full-flavoured fruit juice, for each egg yolk. Whisk the sauce over a constant heat until frothy.

2 Whisk until the sauce holds a trail on top of the mixture. Serve immediately or whisk until cool.

Baked Custard

Preheat the oven to 180°C/350°F/ Gas 4. Grease an ovenproof dish. Beat together four large (US extra large) eggs, a few drops of vanilla essence (extract) and 15–30ml/1–2 tbsp caster sugar. Whisk in 600ml/1 pint/2½ cups hot milk, then strain into the dish. Stand the dish in a roasting pan half-filled with warm water. Bake for 50–60 minutes.

Dessert Sauces

As well as the popular custards and flavoured white sauces, quick and easy dessert toppings can be made almost instantly from ready-made ingredients, and these are ideal to serve over scoops of ice cream. They could also be served with pancakes and are particularly popular with children.

How to Use Vanilla Pods

Vanilla pods (beans) are commonly used in sweet dessert sauces, but they are occasionally used to flavour delicate savoury cream sauces.

To flavour sugar, bury a vanilla pod in a jar of caster (superfine) sugar. It can be used as vanilla-flavoured sugar to add to sweet sauces and desserts.

To infuse (steep) vanilla flavour into milk or cream, heat it gently with the vanilla pod over a low heat until almost boiling. Remove from the heat, cover and leave to stand for 10 minutes. Remove the pod, rinse and dry; it may be re-used several times in this way.

To get maximum flavour from the pod, use a sharp knife to slit the pod length-wise and open out. Use the tip of the knife to scrape out the sticky black seeds inside and add to the hot sauce.

Speedy Sauces for Topping Ice Cream

Lots of store-cupboard (pantry) ingredients can be quickly transformed into sauces to spoon on top of ice cream, so you'll always have a quick dessert.

Marshmallow Melt

Melt 90g/3½ oz marshmallows with 30ml/2 tbsp milk or cream in a small pan. Add a little grated nutmeg and spoon over ice cream.

Black Forest Sauce

Drain a can of black cherries, reserving the juice. Blend a little of the juice with a little arrowroot or cornflour (cornstarch). Add the cornflour mixture to the remaining juice in a pan. Stir over a moderate heat until boiling and lightly thickened, then add the cherries and a dash of kirsch. Bubble for a few seconds, then spoon over the ice cream and top with grated chocolate.

Chocolate-toffee Sauce

Chop a Mars (Heath) bar and heat gently in a pan, stirring until just melted. Spoon over scoops of vanilla ice cream and sprinkle with chopped nuts.

Marmalade Whisky Sauce

Heat 60ml/4 tbsp chunky marmalade in a pan with 30ml/2 tbsp whisky, until just melted. Allow to bubble for a few seconds then spoon over ice cream.

Whisky Sauce

Measure 600ml/1 pint/2½ cups milk. Mix together 30ml/2 tbsp cornflour (cornstarch) with 15ml/1 tbsp of the milk. Bring the remaining milk to a boil, remove from the heat and pour a little on the cornflour mixture. Return the mixture to the pan and heat gently, stirring constantly, until thickened. Simmer for 2 minutes.

Remove from the heat and stir in 30ml/2 tbsp caster (superfine) sugar and 60–90ml/4–6 tbsp whisky.

Presentation Ideas

When you've made a delicious sauce for a special dessert, why not make more of it by using it for decoration on the plate, too? Try one of the following simple ideas to make your sauce into a talking point. Individual slices of desserts, cakes or tarts, or a stuffed baked peach, look especially good like this.

Marbling

Use this technique when you have two contrasting sauces of similar thickness, such as a fruit purée with custard or cream. Spoon alternate spoonfuls of the sauces into a bowl or on to a serving plate, then stir the two sauces lightly together, swirling to create a marbled effect.

Yin-Yang Sauces

This is ideal for two contrasting colours of purée or coulis, such as a raspberry and a mango fruit coulis. Spoon one sauce on each side of a serving plate and push them together gently with a spoon, swirling one around the other, to make a yin-yang shape.

Drizzling

Pour a smooth sauce or coulis into a piping (pastry) bag with a fine pouring lip. Drizzle the sauce in droplets or a fine wavy line on to the plate around the food.

Piping Outlines

Spoon a small amount of fruit coulis or chocolate sauce into a piping bag with a plain writing nozzle. Pipe the outline of a shape on to a serving plate, then spoon in sauce to fill the inside.

Feathering Hearts

Flood the plate with a smooth sauce such as fruit purée. Add small droplets of pouring cream into it at intervals. Draw the tip of a small knife through the cream, to drag each drop into a heart.

Quick Sauces for Crêpes

Rich Butterscotch Sauce

Heat 75g/3oz/6 tbsp butter, 175g/6oz/1½ cups brown sugar and 30ml/2 tbsp golden (light corn) syrup in a pan over a low heat until melted. Remove from the heat and add 75ml/5 tbsp double (heavy) cream, stirring constantly, until smooth. If you like, add about 50g/2oz/½ cup chopped walnuts. Serve hot with ice cream and crêpes or waffles.

Orange Sauce

Melt 25g/1oz/2 tbsp unsalted (sweet) butter in a heavy pan. Stir in 50g/2oz/¼ cup caster (superfine) sugar and cook until golden. Add the juice of two oranges and half a lemon and stir until the caramel has dissolved.

Summer Berries

Melt 25g/1oz/2 tbsp butter in a frying pan. Add in 50g/2oz/¼ cup caster (superfine) sugar and cook until golden. Add the juice of two oranges and the rind of ½ orange and cook until syrupy. Add 350g/12oz/3 cups berries and heat. Add 45ml/3 tbsp Grand Marnier and set alight. Spoon over the crêpes.

Fruit Sauces

From the simplest fresh fruit purée, to a cooked and thickened fruit sauce, there are hundreds of ways to add flavour to desserts, tarts and pies. The addition of a little liqueur or lemon juice can bring out the fruit flavour and prevent discoloration. Some fruit sauces, notably apple and cranberry, partner meat and poultry dishes, and fresh fruit salsas can be eaten to cool down spicy hot dishes.

Making a Fruit Coulis

A delicious fruit coulis will add a sophisticated splash of colour and flavour to desserts and ices. It can be made from either fresh or frozen fruit, in any season. Soft fruits and berries such as raspberries, blackcurrants or strawberries are ideal, and tropical fruits like mango and kiwi fruit can be quickly transformed into exotically flavoured coulis. A few drops of orange flower water or rose water will give a scented flavour, but use it with caution – too much will overpower delicate ingredients.

Remove any hulls, stems, peel or stones (pits) from the fruit.

2 Place the prepared fruit in a blender or food processor and process until smooth.

3 Press the purée through a fine sieve, to remove the pips (seeds) or fibrous parts. Sweeten to taste with icing (confectioners') sugar, and if necessary add a squeeze of lemon juice to sharpen the flavour.

COOK'S TIP

For cooked peeled fruit, mash with a potato masher for a coarser purée.

Peach Sauce

Purée a 400g/14oz can of peaches, together with their juice and 1.5ml/¼ tsp almond essence (extract) in a blender or food processor; chill the sauce before serving with fruit tarts or cakes.

Passion Fruit Coulis

Cut three ripe papayas in half and scoop out the seeds. Peel them and cut the flesh into chunks. Thread the chunks on bamboo skewers.

1 Halve eight passion fruit and scoop out the flesh. Purée in a blender for a few seconds.

2 Press the pulp through a sieve and discard the seeds. Add 30ml/2 tbsp of lime juice, 30ml/2 tbsp of icing (confectioners') sugar and 30ml/2 tbsp of white rum. Stir well until the sugar has dissolved.

3 Spoon some of the coulis on to a serving plate. Place the skewers on top. Drizzle the remaining coulis over the skewers and garnish with a little toasted coconut, if you like.

Chocolate Sauces

Chocolate sauces are enduringly popular, from simple custards to richly indulgent versions combined with liqueur or cream. They can be served with ice cream and other frozen desserts, but are also delicious with poached pears and a wide range of puddings. Flavoured liqueurs can be chosen to echo the flavour of the dessert, and coffee, brandy and cinnamon all go especially well with chocolate.

The more cocoa solids chocolate contains, the stronger the flavour will be. Plain (semisweet) chocolate may have between 30–70 per cent of cocoa solids. Dark (bittersweet) chocolate has around 75 per cent, so if you're aiming for a really rich, dark sauce, this is the best choice. Milk chocolate is much sweeter, containing 20 per cent cocoa solids.

White chocolate contains no cocoa solids, so strictly speaking it is not a chocolate at all, but gets its flavour from cocoa butter.

The best method of melting chocolate is in a double boiler or in a bowl over a pan of hot water. Never allow water or steam to come into contact with the chocolate as this may cause it to stiffen. Overheating will also spoil the flavour and texture. Plain chocolate should not be heated above 49°C/120°F, and milk or white chocolate not above 43°C/110°F.

For sauce recipes where the chocolate is melted with a quantity of other liquid, such as milk or cream, the chocolate may be melted with the liquid in a pan over direct heat, providing there is plenty of liquid. Heat gently, stirring until melted.

Cocoa is ground from the whole cocoa mass after most of the cocoa butter has been extracted.

Creamy Chocolate Sauce

Place 120ml/4fl oz/½ cup double (heavy) cream in a pan and add 130g/4½oz chocolate pieces. Stir over a low heat until the chocolate has melted. Serve warm or cold.

COOK'S TIP

If you run out of chocolate for a sauce recipe, you can use unsweetened cocoa as a substitute. Mix 45ml/3 tbsp cocoa with 15ml/1 tbsp melted butter to replace each 25g/1oz chocolate.

Chocolate Custard Sauce

Melt 90g/3½oz dark (bittersweet) chocolate.

2 Heat 200ml/7fl oz/scant 1 cup *crème anglaise* until hot but not boiling and stir in the melted chocolate until evenly mixed. Serve hot or cold.

Rich Chocolate Brandy Sauce

Break up 115g/4oz plain (semisweet) chocolate into a bowl over a pan of hot water, then heat gently until melted. Remove from the heat and add 30ml/2 tbsp brandy and 30ml/2 tbsp melted butter, then stir until smooth. Serve hot.

Classic Sauces

A comprehensive collection of sauce recipes must, by definition, include as its foundation the traditional, classic recipes that have been handed down through many generations of cooks.

Every country has its enduring time-honoured sauces, from French favourites, such as elegant béchamel sauce, and rich, brown Espagnole sauce, to British favourites such as horseradish or bread sauce; from all-American cranberry sauce to vibrant fresh Italian pesto. Each has evolved from the imaginative use of local foods and has been created to enhance the flavours of the traditional cuisine of the country.

These tried and tested classics form the basis of a repertoire essential to every professional cook. They encompass all of the sauce-making techniques, such as flour-thickened roux and rich emulsions, and some of them form an integral part of world-famous dishes.

In the past, the art of sauce-making required that stocks and other ingredients were prepared entirely by hand, but cooks today have electric mixers and food processors to assist them. The substitution of commercial stock can also save time and effort, and still provide the busy cook with an impressive result, complementing the flavour of both plain and rich cooking.

Béchamel Sauce

THIS IS A CREAMY white sauce with an excellent, mellow flavour, which makes it ideal for lasagne as well as a suitable base or accompaniment for many fish, egg and vegetable dishes.

Serves 4

INGREDIENTS

1 small onion
1 small carrot
1 celery stick
bouquet garni
6 black peppercorns
pinch of freshly grated nutmeg or
*   a blade of mace*
300ml/½ pint/1¼ cups milk
25g/1oz/2 tbsp butter
25g/1oz/¼ cup plain (all-purpose) flour
30ml/2 tbsp single (light) cream
salt and ground black pepper

1 Peel and finely chop the vegetables. Put the vegetables, flavourings and milk in a pan. Bring to the boil. Remove from the heat, cover and allow to infuse (steep) for 30 minutes.

2 Over a gentle heat, melt the butter in a pan, remove from the heat and stir in the flour. Return to the heat and cook for 1–2 minutes, stirring, to make a roux.

3 Reheat the flavoured milk until almost boiling. Strain into a jug (pitcher), pressing the vegetables with the back of a spoon.

4 Off the heat, gradually blend the milk into the roux, stirring vigorously after each addition. Bring to the boil and stir constantly until the sauce thickens. Simmer gently for 3–4 minutes.

5 Remove the pan from the heat. Season with salt and pepper to taste and stir in the cream.

Basic White Sauce

THIS WHITE SAUCE IS wonderfully adaptable for all kinds of savoury dishes, but it can be bland so always taste and season carefully.

Serves 6

INGREDIENTS
600ml/1 pint/2½ cups milk
25g/1oz/2 tbsp butter
25g/1oz/¼ cup plain (all-purpose) flour
salt and ground black pepper

1 Warm the milk in a pan over a low heat, but do not boil.

2 In a separate pan melt the butter, then stir in the flour and cook gently for 1–2 minutes to make a roux. Do not allow it to brown.

3 Remove the pan from the heat, gradually blend in the milk, stirring vigorously after each addition to prevent lumps forming.

4 Return to the heat and bring to the boil slowly, stirring constantly until the sauce thickens.

5 Simmer gently for a further 3–4 minutes until thickened and smooth. Season with salt and ground black pepper to taste.

COOK'S TIPS

• For a thicker, coating sauce, increase the amount of flour to 50g/2oz/½ cup and the butter to 50g/2oz/¼ cup.
• If you aren't using a non-stick pan, use a small whisk to incorporate the flour and milk smoothly.

VARIATIONS

• Parsley sauce is traditionally served with bacon, fish and broad (fava) beans. Stir in 15ml/1 tbsp chopped fresh parsley just before serving.
• Cheese sauce makes delicious egg and vegetable gratins. Stir in 50g/2oz/½ cup finely grated mature (sharp) Cheddar and 2.5ml/½ tsp prepared mustard.

Velouté Sauce

THIS SAVOURY POURING SAUCE is named after its smooth, velvety texture. It's based on a white stock made from fish, vegetables or meat, so it can easily be adapted to the dish you are serving.

Serves 4

INGREDIENTS

600ml/1 pint/2½ cups stock
25g/1oz/2 tbsp butter
25g/1oz/¼ cup plain (all-purpose) flour
30ml/2 tbsp single (light) cream
salt and ground black pepper

1 Heat the stock until almost boiling, but do not boil. In another pan melt the butter and stir in the flour. Cook, stirring, over a moderate heat for 3–4 minutes, or until a pale, straw colour, stirring constantly.

2 Remove the pan from the heat and gradually blend in the hot stock. Return to the heat and bring to the boil, stirring constantly, until the sauce thickens.

3 Continue to cook at a very slow simmer, stirring occasionally, until reduced by about one-quarter.

4 Skim the surface during cooking to remove any scum, or pour through a very fine strainer.

5 Just before serving, remove from the heat and stir in the cream. Season to taste.

VARIATION

For a richer flavour in a special dish, replace 30–45ml/2–3 tbsp of the stock with dry white wine or vermouth.

Lemon Sauce with Tarragon

THE SHARPNESS OF LEMON and the mild aniseed flavour of tarragon add zest to chicken, egg or steamed vegetable dishes.

Serves 4

INGREDIENTS

1 lemon
a small bunch of fresh tarragon
1 shallot, finely chopped
90ml/6 tbsp white wine
1 quantity Velouté sauce
45ml/3 tbsp double (heavy) cream
30ml/2 tbsp brandy
salt and ground black pepper

1 Thinly pare the rind from the lemon, taking care not to remove any of the white pith. Squeeze the juice from the lemon and pour it into a pan. Discard the lemon.

2 Discard the coarse stalks from the tarragon. Chop the leaves and add all but 15ml/1 tbsp to the pan with the lemon rind and shallot.

3 Add the wine and simmer gently until the liquid is reduced by half. Strain into a clean pan.

4 Add the Velouté sauce, cream, brandy and reserved tarragon. Heat through, taste and adjust the seasoning if necessary.

COOK'S TIP

This sauce goes well with pieces of boned chicken breast portions, wrapped with streaky (fatty) bacon rashers (strips) and grilled (broiled) or pan-fried.

Espagnole Sauce

ESPAGNOLE IS A CLASSIC rich brown sauce, ideal for serving with red meat and game. It also makes a delicious, full-flavoured base for other sauces.

Serves 4–6

INGREDIENTS

25g/1oz/2 tbsp butter
50g/2oz bacon, chopped
2 shallots, unpeeled and chopped
1 carrot, chopped
1 celery stick, chopped
mushroom trimmings (if available)
25g/1oz/¼ cup plain (all-purpose) flour
600ml/1 pint/2½ cups hot brown stock
bouquet garni
30ml/2 tbsp tomato purée (paste)
15ml/1 tbsp sherry (optional)
salt and ground black pepper

1 Melt the butter in a heavy pan and fry the bacon for 2–3 minutes. Add the shallots, carrot, celery and mushroom trimmings, if using, and cook the mixture for a further 5–6 minutes, or until golden.

2 Gradually stir in the flour and cook for 5–10 minutes over a medium heat until the roux has become a rich brown colour.

3 Remove the pan from the heat and gradually blend in the stock.

4 Slowly bring to the boil, continuing to stir until the sauce thickens. Add the bouquet garni, tomato purée, sherry, if using, and seasoning. Reduce the heat and simmer gently for 1 hour, stirring occasionally.

5 Strain the Espagnole sauce, and gently reheat before serving.

COOK'S TIP

This sauce can be covered and stored in the refrigerator for up to 4 days, or it can be frozen for up to 1 month. It's worth making double the quantity and keeping a batch in reserve.

Chasseur Sauce

THIS EXCELLENT MUSHROOM and wine sauce will transform simple pan-fried or grilled chicken, grilled or roast pork, or rabbit dishes. To give the sauce more flavour use chestnut mushrooms.

Serves 3–4

INGREDIENTS

25g/1oz/2 tbsp butter
1 shallot, finely chopped
115g/4oz/2 cups mushrooms, sliced
120ml/4fl oz/½ cup white wine
30ml/2 tbsp brandy
1 quantity Espagnole sauce
15ml/1 tbsp chopped fresh tarragon
   or chervil

1 Melt the butter in a medium or large pan over a medium heat, and fry the shallot until soft but not brown.

2 Add the mushrooms and sauté, stirring occasionally until they just begin to brown.

3 Pour in the wine and brandy, and simmer over a medium heat until reduced by half.

4 Add the Espagnole sauce and herbs and heat through, stirring occasionally. Serve hot.

Tangy Orange Sauce

KNOWN AS *SAUCE BIGARADE*, this is the perfect accompaniment for roast duckling and rich game. For a full mellow flavour it is best made with the rich roasting-pan juices.

Serves 4–6

INGREDIENTS

roasting-pan juices or 25g/1oz/
  2 tbsp butter
40g/1½oz/⅓ cup plain (all-purpose) flour
300ml/½ pint hot stock (preferably duck)
150ml/¼ pint/⅔ cup red wine
2 Seville (Temple) oranges or 2 sweet
  oranges plus 10ml/2 tsp lemon juice
15ml/1 tbsp orange-flavoured liqueur
30ml/2 tbsp redcurrant jelly
salt and ground black pepper

1 Carefully pour off any excess fat from the roasting pan, leaving the rich meat juices behind, or melt the butter in a small pan.

2 Sprinkle the flour into the juices or butter and cook, stirring constantly, for about 4 minutes, or until the mixture is lightly browned.

3 Off the heat, gradually blend in the hot stock and wine. Return to the heat and bring to the boil, stirring constantly. Lower the heat and simmer gently for 5 minutes.

4 Meanwhile, using a citrus zester, peel the rind thinly from one orange. Squeeze the juice from both of the oranges.

5 Place the rind in a small pan, cover with boiling water and bring back to the boil. Simmer for 5 minutes, then strain and add the rind to the sauce.

6 Add the orange juice to the sauce, along with the lemon juice, if using, and the liqueur and jelly. Stir until the jelly has dissolved. Season with salt and pepper to taste.

COOK'S TIP

Seville (Temple) oranges have a distinctive bitter flavour, which is good for savoury dishes, but they have a short season. They can be frozen whole, or you can freeze the juice and rind separately.

Hollandaise Sauce

A RICH BUTTER SAUCE rather like a
warm mayonnaise, is perfect for
steamed or grilled fish, such as
salmon, or vegetables such as
broccoli, asparagus or new potatoes.
The secret of success is patience.

Serves 2–3

INGREDIENTS

30ml/2 tbsp white wine or tarragon vinegar
15ml/1 tbsp water
6 black peppercorns
1 bay leaf
115g/4oz/½ cup butter
2 egg yolks
salt and ground black pepper
15–30ml/1–2 tbsp single (light)
    cream (optional)

1 Place the vinegar, water, peppercorns,
and bay leaf in a pan. Simmer the
liquid gently until it has reduced by half.
Strain and allow to cool.

2 In a separate bowl, cream the
butter until soft.

3 In a double boiler, or a heatproof
bowl sitting over a pan of gently
simmering, but not boiling, water, whisk
the egg yolks and infused (steeped)
vinegar liquid together gently until the
mixture is light and fluffy.

4 Gradually add the butter a tiny
piece at a time – about the size of
a hazelnut will be enough. Whisk
quickly until all the butter has been
absorbed before adding any more.

5 Season lightly and, if the sauce is
too sharp, add a little more butter.

6 For a thinner version of the sauce,
stir in some single cream. Serve
immediately.

COOK'S TIP

*Any leftover sauce can be stored in the
refrigerator for up to a week. Reheat very
gently in a bowl over simmering water,
whisking constantly.*

Mousseline Sauce

A TRULY LUSCIOUS SAUCE, which is subtly flavoured, rich and creamy. Try serving it as a dip for prepared artichokes or artichoke hearts, or with shellfish.

Serves 4

INGREDIENTS

2 egg yolks
15ml/1 tbsp lemon juice
75g/3oz/6 tbsp softened butter
90ml/6 tbsp double (heavy) cream
extra lemon juice (optional)
salt and ground black pepper

1 To make the sauce, whisk the yolks and lemon juice in a bowl over a pan of barely simmering water, or a double boiler, until very thick and fluffy.

2 Whisk in the butter, but only a very little at a time, until it is thoroughly absorbed and the sauce has the consistency of mayonnaise.

3 In a separate bowl, whisk the cream until it forms stiff peaks. Fold into the warm sauce and adjust the seasoning. You can add a little more lemon juice for extra sharpness.

VARIATION

For a lavish accompaniment to special fish dishes such as lobster or Dover sole, stir in 30–45ml/2–3 tbsp caviar before serving as a Caviar Mousseline.

Béarnaise Sauce

FOR DEDICATED MEAT EATERS, this herby butter sauce adds a note of sophistication without swamping your grilled or pan-fried steak. It also enhances plain vegetables.

Serves 2–3

INGREDIENTS

45ml/3 tbsp white wine vinegar
30ml/2 tbsp water
1 small onion, finely chopped
a few fresh tarragon and chervil sprigs
1 bay leaf
6 crushed black peppercorns
115g/4oz/½ cup butter
2 egg yolks
15ml/1 tbsp chopped fresh herbs,
    such as tarragon, parsley, chervil
salt and ground black pepper

1 Place the vinegar, water, onion, herb sprigs, bay leaf and peppercorns in a pan. Simmer gently until the liquid is reduced by half. Strain and cool.

2 In a separate bowl, cream the butter until soft.

3 In a bowl over a pan of gently simmering water, or a double boiler, whisk the egg yolks and liquid until light and fluffy.

4 Gradually add the butter, half a teaspoonful at a time. Whisk until all the butter has been incorporated before adding any more.

5 Add the chopped fresh herbs and season to taste.

6 Serve warm, not hot, on the side of a grilled (broiled) steak or allow a good spoonful to melt over new potatoes.

VARIATION

To make Choron sauce, which is very good with roast or grilled lamb, stir in 15ml/1 tbsp tomato purée (paste) to the sauce at the end of step 1.

Newburg Sauce

THIS CREAMY MADEIRA-FLAVOURED sauce originated in America. Its rich flavour will not mask delicate foods and so it is ideal for serving with shellfish or chicken.

Serves 4

INGREDIENTS

15g/½oz/1 tbsp butter
1 small shallot, finely chopped
pinch of cayenne pepper
300ml/½ pint/1¼ cups double
    (heavy) cream
60ml/4 tbsp Madeira
3 egg yolks
salt and ground black pepper

1 Melt the butter in a heatproof bowl placed over a pan of simmering water, or in a double boiler.

2 Add the chopped shallot to the butter and cook gently until it is soft and transparent.

3 Add the cayenne and all but 60ml/ 4 tbsp of the cream. Leave over the simmering water for 10 minutes to reduce slightly.

4 Stir in the Madeira. Beat the yolks with the remaining cream and stir into the hot sauce. Continue stirring the sauce over barely simmering water until thickened. Season to taste. Serve immediately.

COOK'S TIPS

• To give the sauce a luxurious festive look, stir in 15–30ml/1–2 tbsp of pink or black lumpfish roe at the end of cooking.
• Spoon over fish, shellfish or chicken, reserving some for pouring, and serve immediately. Garnish the dish with fresh herbs.

Pesto Sauce

THERE IS NOTHING MORE evocative of the warmth of Italy than a good home-made pesto. Serve in generous spoonfuls with your favourite pasta.

Serves 3–4

INGREDIENTS

50g/2oz/1 cup basil leaves
2 garlic cloves, crushed
30ml/2 tbsp pine nuts
120ml/4fl oz/½ cup olive oil
40g/1½ oz/½ cup finely grated fresh
   Parmesan cheese
salt and ground black pepper

By hand: Using a mortar and pestle, grind the basil, garlic, pine nuts and seasoning to a fine paste.

2 Transfer the mixture to a bowl and whisk in the oil a little at a time.

3 Add the cheese and blend well. Adjust the seasoning to taste and heat the sauce gently.

Using a food processor: Place the basil, garlic, pine nuts and seasoning in the food processor and process as finely as possible.

2 With the machine running slowly add the oil in a thin stream, combining the ingredients until they have formed a smooth paste.

3 Add the cheese and pulse quickly three or four times. Adjust the seasoning if necessary and heat gently.

VARIATION

Pesto makes an excellent dressing for boiled new potatoes. Serve while hot or allow to cool to room temperature.

Rich Tomato Sauce

FOR A FULL TOMATO flavour and rich red colour, fresh Italian plum tomatoes are an excellent choice if they are available.

Serves 4–6

INGREDIENTS

30ml/2 tbsp olive oil
1 large onion, chopped
2 garlic cloves, crushed
1 carrot, finely chopped
1 celery stick, finely chopped
675g/1½lb tomatoes, peeled and chopped
150ml/¼ pint/⅔ cup red wine
150ml/¼ pint/⅔ cup vegetable stock
bouquet garni
2.5–5ml/½–1 tsp sugar
15ml/1 tbsp tomato purée (paste)
salt and ground black pepper

1 Heat the oil in a pan, add the onion and garlic and sauté until soft and pale golden brown. Add the carrot and celery and continue to cook, stirring occasionally, until golden.

2 Stir in the tomatoes, wine, stock and bouquet garni. Season with salt and ground black pepper to taste.

3 Bring the tomato mixture to the boil, then cover and simmer gently for 45 minutes, stirring occasionally to avoid burning. Remove the bouquet garni from the liquid, taste the sauce and adjust the seasoning, adding a pinch of sugar and tomato purée as necessary.

4 Serve the sauce as it is or, for a smoother texture, press through a sieve, or purée in a blender or food processor. This is delicious spooned over sliced courgettes (zucchini) or whole green beans.

Blue Cheese and Walnut Sauce

THIS IS A VERY quick but indulgently creamy sauce. The blue cheese melts with cream to make a simple sauce to serve with vegetables or pasta.

Serves 2

INGREDIENTS

50g/2oz/¼ cup butter
50g/2oz/¾ cup button (white)
  mushrooms, sliced
150g/5oz hard blue cheese, such as
  Gorgonzola, Stilton or Danish Blue
150ml/¼ pint/⅔ cup sour cream
25g/1oz/⅓ cup grated Pecorino cheese
50g/2oz/⅓ cup broken walnut pieces
salt and ground black pepper

1 Melt the butter in a pan, add the mushrooms and gently fry for 3–5 minutes, stirring occasionally until lightly browned.

2 Place the blue cheese and cream in a bowl, add seasoning to taste, and mash together well using a fork.

3 Stir the cheese mixture into the mushroom mixture and heat gently, stirring, until melted.

4 Finally, stir in the Pecorino cheese and the walnut pieces. Serve warm.

Quick Satay Sauce

THERE ARE MANY VERSIONS of this tasty peanut sauce. This one is very speedy and it tastes delicious drizzled over grilled or barbecued skewers of chicken. For parties, spear chunks of chicken with cocktail sticks and arrange around a bowl of sauce.

Serves 4

INGREDIENTS

200ml/7fl oz/scant 1 cup coconut cream
60ml/4 tbsp crunchy peanut butter
1 tsp Worcestershire sauce
Tabasco sauce, to taste
fresh coconut, to garnish (optional)

1 Pour the coconut cream into a small pan and heat it gently over a low heat for about 2 minutes.

2 Add the peanut butter and stir vigorously until it is blended into the coconut cream. Continue to heat until the mixture is warm but not boiling hot.

3 Add the Worcestershire sauce and a dash of Tabasco to taste. Pour into a serving bowl.

COOK'S TIP

Thick coconut milk can be substituted for coconut cream, but take care to buy an unsweetened variety for this recipe.

4 Use a potato peeler to shave thin curls from a piece of fresh coconut, if using. Sprinkle the coconut over the dish of your choice and serve immediately with the sauce.

Green Peppercorn Sauce

THIS SAUCE IS EXCELLENT with pasta, pork steaks or grilled chicken. The green peppercorns in brine are a better choice than the dry-packed type because they tend to give a more rounded flavour.

Serves 3–4

INGREDIENTS

15ml/1 tbsp green peppercorns in
   brine, drained
1 small onion, finely chopped
25g/1oz/2 tbsp butter
300ml/½ pint/1¼ cups light stock
juice of ½ lemon
15ml/1 tbsp beurre manié
45ml/3 tbsp double (heavy) cream
5ml/1 tsp Dijon mustard
salt and ground black pepper

1 Dry the peppercorns on absorbent kitchen paper, then crush lightly under the blade of a heavy-duty knife or use a mortar and pestle.

2 Soften the onion in the butter, add the stock and lemon juice and simmer for 15 minutes.

3 Whisk in the beurre manié a little at a time and continue to cook, stirring, until the sauce thickens.

VARIATION

For a lighter, less rich sauce, use crème fraîche instead of the double cream.

4 Reduce the heat and stir in the peppercorns, cream and mustard. Heat until boiling then season to taste. Serve hot with buttered pasta or the dish of your choice.

COOK'S TIP

For beurre manié, knead together equal quantities of butter and flour.

Barbecue Sauce

BRUSH THIS SAUCE OVER chops, kebabs or chicken drumsticks before cooking on the barbecue, or serve as a hot or cold accompaniment to hot dogs and burgers.

Serves 4

INGREDIENTS

30ml/2 tbsp vegetable oil
1 large onion, chopped
2 garlic cloves, crushed
400g/14oz can tomatoes
30ml/2 tbsp Worcestershire sauce
15ml/1 tbsp white wine vinegar
45ml/3 tbsp honey
5ml/1 tsp mustard powder
2.5ml/½ tsp chilli seasoning or mild chilli powder
salt and ground black pepper

1 In a pan, heat the oil and fry the onion and garlic until soft.

2 Stir in the remaining ingredients and bring to the boil. Simmer, uncovered, for 15–20 minutes, stirring occasionally. Cool slightly.

3 Pour into a food processor or blender and process until smooth.

4 Press the sauce through a sieve if you prefer a smoother result, and adjust the seasoning with salt and pepper to taste before serving.

VARIATION

For a really rich, spicy chilli flavour, omit the chilli seasoning and instead add a small red chilli, seeded and chopped. Leave the seeds in if you like it really hot.

Apple Sauce

REALLY MORE OF A condiment than a sauce, this tart purée is usually served cold or warm, rather than hot. It's typically served with rice, roast pork or duck, but is also good with cold meats and savoury pies.

Serves 6

INGREDIENTS

225g/8oz tart cooking apples
30ml/2 tbsp water
thin strip of lemon rind
15ml/1 tbsp butter
15–30ml/1–2 tbsp caster (superfine) sugar

1 Peel the apples, cut into quarters and remove the core. Cut into thin, even slices.

2 Place the apples in a pan with the water and lemon rind. Cook, uncovered, over a low heat until very soft, stirring occasionally.

3 Remove the lemon rind from the pan and discard. Beat the apples to a pulp with a spoon, or press through a sieve.

VARIATIONS

• *To make a Normandy Apple Sauce, try stirring in 15ml/1 tbsp Calvados with the butter and sugar at step 4.*
• *To make a creamy savoury apple sauce, stir in 30ml/2 tbsp sour cream or crème fraîche at step 4.*

4 Stir the butter into the apple sauce and then add sugar to taste.

Mint Sauce

TART, YET SWEET, this simple sauce is the perfect foil to rich meat. It's best served, of course, with the new season's tender roast lamb, but it is also wonderful with grilled lamb chops or pan-fried duck.

Serves 6

INGREDIENTS
small bunch of mint
15ml/1 tbsp sugar
30ml/2 tbsp boiling water
45ml/3 tbsp white wine vinegar

1 Strip the mint leaves from the stalks and finely chop the leaves.

2 Place in a bowl with the sugar and pour on the boiling water. Stir well and allow the mixture to stand for 5–10 minutes.

3 Add the vinegar and leave to stand for 1–2 hours before serving.

COOK'S TIP

This sauce also makes a refreshing dressing to enhance the summery flavour of fresh peas or new potatoes.

Cranberry Sauce

THIS IS THE TRADITIONAL sauce for roast turkey, but don't keep it just for festive occasions. The vibrant colour and tart taste are a perfect partner to any white roast meat, and it makes a great addition to a chicken or Brie sandwich.

Serves 6

INGREDIENTS
1 orange
225g/8oz/2 cups cranberries
250g/9oz/1¼ cups caster (superfine) sugar
150ml/¼ pint/⅔ cup water

1 Pare the rind thinly from the orange using a swivel-bladed vegetable peeler, taking care not to remove any white pith. Squeeze the juice.

2 Place in a pan with the cranberries, sugar and water.

3 Bring to a boil, stirring until the sugar has dissolved, then allow to simmer gently for 10–15 minutes or until the berries burst.

4 Remove the orange rind and allow to cool before serving.

COOK'S TIP

Fresh or frozen cranberries may be used in this sauce, depending on the season. Use fresh as a first choice.

Horseradish Sauce

THIS LIGHT, CREAMY SAUCE has a peppery flavour that's spiced with just a hint of mustard. It is the classic accompaniment to roast beef, but is perfect, too, with herby sausages and grilled fish, especially oily fish such as mackerel.

Serves 6

INGREDIENTS

7.5cm/3in piece fresh horseradish
15ml/1 tbsp lemon juice
10ml/2 tsp sugar
2.5ml/½ tsp English (hot) mustard powder
150ml/¼ pint/⅔ cup double (heavy) cream

1 Scrub and peel the piece of fresh horseradish, and then grate it as finely as possible.

2 In a bowl, mix together the grated horseradish, lemon juice, sugar and mustard powder.

3 Whip the cream until it stands in soft peaks, then gently fold in the horseradish mixture.

VARIATION

For a change of flavour, replace the lemon juice with tarragon vinegar.

Bread Sauce

SMOOTH AND SURPRISINGLY DELICATE, this old-fashioned sauce dates back to medieval times. It's traditionally served with roast chicken, turkey and game birds.

Serves 6

INGREDIENTS

1 small onion
4 cloves
bay leaf
300ml/½ pint/1¼ cups milk
90g/3½ oz/scant 2 cups fresh
   white breadcrumbs
15ml/1 tbsp butter
15ml/1 tbsp single (light) cream
salt and ground black pepper

1 Peel the onion and stick the cloves into it. Put it into a pan with the bay leaf and pour in the milk.

2 Bring to the boil, then remove from the heat and allow to infuse (steep) for 15–20 minutes. Remove the bay leaf and onion from the milk.

3 Return to the heat and stir in the breadcrumbs. Simmer for 4–5 minutes, or until thick and creamy.

4 Stir in the butter and cream, then season to taste.

COOK'S TIP

If you would prefer a less strong flavour, reduce the number of cloves in the onion to one or two and add a little freshly grated nutmeg to the milk instead.

Sauces for Pasta Dishes

There's a wealth of sauce recipes for all types of pasta, and not surprisingly they are often Italian in origin. Endlessly varied in style, they may be delicate, buttery herb mixtures or rich cream sauces, hearty meat ragùs or chunky vegetable sauces. Many are based on tomatoes from southern Italy, and make the very best use of those other Mediterranean flavours – olive oil, garlic and basil – all classic partners for pasta.

Most pasta sauces are refreshingly simple and foolproof, and do not need hours of preparation. Most are cooked in a matter of minutes, retaining all the natural flavours of fresh ingredients, with the exception of long-simmered rich meat and tomato ragùs, which by tradition are simmered at length on a low flame for a more concentrated, mature flavour.

Many of these sauces are designed to match particular types or shapes of pasta, but there are no hard and fast rules. Many of the sauces work well with other types of pasta, so try experimenting with your favourites.

It's rare for a pasta sauce to be flour-thickened, but many are enriched or thickened with eggs, such as carbonara. Those that are simmered over long periods, such as Bolognese sauce, reach a thicker consistency as they are reduced and become more concentrated. Many form an integral part of the dish, and may be as simple as olive oil with Parmesan cheese and herbs. The choice is yours.

Making Pasta Dough

Home-made pasta has a wonderfully light, almost silky texture – quite different from the so-called fresh pasta that you buy in the shops. If you use egg in the mixture, which is recommended if you are making pasta at home, the dough is easy to make and the initial process is not that different from making bread.

Pasta with Eggs

INGREDIENTS

300g/11oz/2¾ cups flour
3 eggs
5ml/1 tsp salt

COOK'S TIP

Don't skimp on the kneading time or the finished pasta will not be light and silky.

1 Mound the flour on a clean surface and make a large, deep well in the centre with your hands. Keep the sides of the well so that when the eggs are added they will stay in the well.

2 Crack the eggs into the well and add the salt. With a table knife, mix the eggs and salt together, then gradually incorporate the flour from the sides of the well.

3 As soon as the mixture is no longer liquid, dip your fingers in the flour and work the ingredients into a rough and sticky dough. If the dough is too dry, add a few drops of cold water; if it is too moist, sprinkle a little flour over it.

4 Press the dough into a rough ball and knead it as you would bread. Push it away from you with the heel of your hand, then fold the dough back on itself so that it faces towards you and push it out again.

5 Continue folding the dough back a little further each time and pushing it out until you have folded it back all the way towards you and all the dough has been kneaded. Give the dough a quarter turn anti- (counter) clockwise, then continue kneading, folding and turning for 10 minutes. The dough should be very smooth and elastic.

6 Wrap the dough in clear film (plastic wrap) and leave to rest for 15–20 minutes at room temperature. It will then be ready to roll.

Making Pasta Shapes

1 Unwrap the dough and cut it in half. Work on half at once.

2 Sprinkle flour on the work surface, add the dough and flatten it.

3 Roll out until it is 3mm/⅛in thick. It is now ready to cut into pasta shapes.

Italian Plum Tomato Sauce with Cheese and Ham Ravioli

THIS TASTY SAUCE USES pantry ingredients, which saves time if you have an elaborate pasta to make. Serve with meat or fish too.

Serves 4–6

INGREDIENTS
500g/1¼lb fresh pasta dough with eggs
60ml/4 tbsp grated fresh Pecorino cheese,
    plus extra to serve

For the filling
175g/6oz ricotta cheese
30ml/2 tbsp grated fresh Parmesan cheese
115g/4oz prosciutto, finely chopped
150g/5oz fresh mozzarella cheese, drained
    and finely chopped
1 small (US medium) egg
15ml/1 tbsp chopped fresh flat leaf parsley,
    plus extra to garnish

For the Italian plum tomato sauce
30ml/2 tbsp olive oil
1 onion, finely chopped
400g/14oz can chopped plum tomatoes
15ml/1 tbsp sun-dried tomato paste
5–10ml/1–2 tsp dried oregano
salt and ground black pepper

1 To make the sauce, heat the oil in a pan, add the onion and cook, stirring frequently, until softened.

2 Add the tomatoes. Fill the empty can with water, pour it into the pan, then stir in the tomato paste, oregano and seasoning to taste. Bring to the boil and stir well, then cover the pan and simmer for 30 minutes, stirring occasionally and adding more water if the sauce becomes too thick.

3 Put the filling ingredients in a bowl and season to taste. Mix with a fork, breaking up the ricotta.

4 Using a pasta machine, roll out one-quarter of the pasta into a 90–100cm/36–40in strip. Cut the strip into two 45–50cm/18–20in lengths.

5 Using two teaspoons, put little mounds of the filling, 10–12 in total, along one side of one of the pasta strips, spacing them evenly. The filling will be quite moist. Brush a little water around each mound, then fold the plain side of the pasta strip over.

6 Starting from the folded edge, press down gently with your fingertips around each mound, pushing the air out at the unfolded edge.

7 Sprinkle lightly with flour. With a fluted pasta wheel, cut along each long side, then in between each mound, to make small square shapes.

8 Put the ravioli on floured dish towels; sprinkle lightly with flour. Allow to dry while repeating the process with the remaining pasta, to give you 80–96 ravioli altogether.

9 Drop the ravioli into a large pan of boiling, lightly salted water, bring the water back to the boil and boil for 4–5 minutes. Drain well. Spoon about one-third of the ravioli into a warmed serving bowl. Sprinkle with 15ml/1 tbsp grated Pecorino and pour over a third of the tomato sauce.

10 Repeat the layers twice, then top with the remaining grated Pecorino. Serve immediately, garnished with chopped parsley.

Tomato and Chilli Sauce with Pasta

THIS IS A SPECIALITY OF LAZIO in Italy
– the Italian name for the sauce,
al arrabbiata, means rabid or angry,
and describes its heat.

Serves 4

INGREDIENTS
300g/11oz dried penne or tortiglioni

For the tomato and chilli sauce
500g/1¼lb sugocasa
2 garlic cloves, crushed
150ml/¼ pint/⅔ cup dry white wine
15ml/1 tbsp sun-dried tomato paste
1 fresh red chilli
30ml/2 tbsp finely chopped fresh flat leaf
  parsley, plus extra to garnish
salt and ground black pepper
grated fresh Pecorino cheese, to serve

1 Put the sugocasa, garlic, wine, tomato
paste and whole chilli in a pan and
bring to the boil. Cover and simmer
over a low heat.

2 Drop the pasta into a large pan of
rapidly boiling lightly salted water
and cook for 10–12 minutes, or until
al dente.

3 Remove the chilli from the sauce
and add the parsley. Taste for
seasoning. If you prefer a hotter taste,
chop some or all of the chilli and
return it to the sauce.

4 Drain the pasta and tip into a
warmed large bowl. Pour the sauce
over the pasta and toss to mix. Serve
at once, sprinkled with parsley and
grated Pecorino.

COOK'S TIPS

• *If you prefer the flavour to be slightly
less hot, remove the seeds from the chilli
before using. Split the chilli down its
length and scrape out the fiery seeds
with the tip of a knife.*
• *Sugocasa literally means "house
sauce" and consists of tomatoes,
crushed coarsely so that they have a
chunky texture.*

Sun-dried Tomato and Radicchio Sauce with Paglia e Fieno

THIS IS A LIGHT, MODERN pasta dish of the kind served in fashionable restaurants. It is the presentation that sets it apart. It is very quick and easy to prepare.

Serves 4

INGREDIENTS

45ml/3 tbsp pine nuts

350g/12oz paglia e fieno pasta

30ml/2 tbsp extra virgin olive oil

4–6 spring onions (scallions), thinly sliced
into rings

For the sun-dried tomato and
radicchio sauce

15ml/1 tbsp extra virgin olive oil

30ml/2 tbsp sun-dried tomato paste

40g/1¹/₂ oz radicchio leaves, finely shredded

salt and ground black pepper

1 Put the pine nuts in a heavy frying pan and toss over a medium heat for 1–2 minutes until lightly toasted and golden brown. Remove and set aside.

2 Cook the pasta according to the packet instructions, keeping the colours separate by using two pans.

3 To make the sauce, heat the oil in a medium frying pan. Add the sun-dried tomato paste, then stir in two ladlefuls of pasta cooking water. Simmer until the sauce is slightly reduced, stirring constantly.

4 Stir in the shredded radicchio, then taste and season. Keep on a low heat. Drain the pasta, keeping the colours separate, and return them to the pans in which they were cooked. Add 15ml/1 tbsp of oil to each pan and toss over a medium to high heat until the pasta is glistening.

5 Arrange a portion of green and white pasta in each of four warmed bowls, then spoon the sun-dried tomato and radicchio sauce in the centre. Sprinkle the spring onions and toasted pine nuts decoratively over the top and serve immediately. Before eating, each diner should toss the sauce with the pasta to mix well.

COOK'S TIP

If you find the presentation too fussy, you can toss the sun-dried tomato and radicchio mixture with the pasta in one large warmed bowl before serving, then sprinkle with spring onions and pine nuts.

Cannelloni with Two Sauces

THE COMBINATION OF THE full-flavoured tomato sauce and the creamy white sauce makes this cannelloni dish a success. For a special occasion, make it in advance to the baking stage. Add the white sauce and bake on the day.

Serves 6

INGREDIENTS

15ml/1 tbsp olive oil
1 small onion, finely chopped
450g/1lb minced (ground) beef
1 garlic clove, finely chopped
5ml/1 tsp dried mixed herbs
120ml/4fl oz/½ cup beef stock
1 egg
75g/3oz cooked ham or mortadella sausage, finely chopped
45ml/3 tbsp fine fresh white breadcrumbs
115g/4oz/1¼ cups freshly grated Parmesan cheese
18 precooked cannelloni tubes
salt and ground black pepper

For the tomato sauce
30ml/2 tbsp olive oil
1 small onion, finely chopped
½ carrot, finely chopped
1 celery stick, finely chopped
1 garlic clove, crushed
400g/14oz can chopped plum tomatoes
a few sprigs of fresh basil
2.5ml/½ tsp dried oregano

For the white sauce
50g/2oz/¼ cup butter
50g/2oz/½ cup plain (all-purpose) flour
900ml/1½ pints/3¾ cups milk
fresh nutmeg

1 Heat the olive oil in a pan and cook the chopped onion over a gentle heat, stirring occasionally, for about 5 minutes, until softened.

2 Add the minced beef and garlic and cook for 10 minutes, stirring and breaking up any lumps with a wooden spoon.

3 Add the herbs, and season to taste, then moisten with half the stock. Cover the pan and allow to simmer for 25 minutes, stirring occasionally and adding more stock as it reduces. Spoon into a bowl and allow to cool.

4 To make the tomato sauce, heat the olive oil in a pan, add the vegetables and garlic and cook over a medium heat, stirring frequently, for 10 minutes. Add the tomatoes. Fill the empty can with water, pour it into the pan, then add the herbs, and season to taste. Bring to a boil, lower the heat, cover and simmer for 25–30 minutes, stirring occasionally. Purée the tomato sauce in a blender or food processor.

5 To the meat, add the egg, ham or mortadella, breadcrumbs and 90ml/6 tbsp of the grated Parmesan, and stir well to mix. Taste for seasoning.

6 Spread a little of the tomato sauce over the bottom of a rectangular ovenproof dish. Using a teaspoon, fill the cannelloni with the meat mixture.

7 Place the cannelloni in a single layer on top of the sauce. Pour the remaining tomato sauce over the top.

8 Preheat the oven to 190°C/375°F/Gas 5. For the white sauce, melt the butter in pan, add the flour and cook for 1–2 minutes. Remove from the heat and blend in the milk.

9 Return to the heat, bring to the boil and stir until smooth and thick. Grate in fresh nutmeg, and season.

10 Pour over the cannelloni, then sprinkle with Parmesan. Bake for 40–45 minutes. Leave to stand for 10 minutes before serving.

Tomato and Courgette Sauce with Tagliatelle

THE TOMATO AND COURGETTE sauce goes well with a variety of pastas and is quick to make.

Serves 3–4

INGREDIENTS
225g/8oz wholewheat tagliatelle

For the tomato and courgette sauce
5–6 ripe plum tomatoes
30ml/2 tbsp olive oil
1 onion, chopped
2 celery sticks, chopped
1 garlic clove, crushed
2 courgettes (zucchini), halved lengthways
    and sliced
30ml/2 tbsp sun-dried tomato paste
salt and ground black pepper

To serve
50g/2oz/½ cup flaked (sliced)
    almonds, toasted

1 To make the sauce, place the tomatoes in a bowl of boiling water for 30 seconds. Peel, then chop.

2 Bring a large pan of lightly salted water to the boil, add the pasta and cook for about 12 minutes, or according to the instructions on the packet, until *al dente*.

3 Meanwhile, heat the oil in another pan and add the chopped onion, celery, garlic and courgettes.

4 Sauté over a gentle heat for 3–4 minutes, until the onions have become lightly browned.

5 Stir in the tomatoes and sun-dried tomato paste. Cook gently for a further 5 minutes, then add salt and pepper to taste.

6 Drain the pasta, return it to the pan and add the sauce. Toss well. Place in a serving dish and sprinkle the toasted almonds over the top to serve.

COOK'S TIP

If using fresh pasta, you'll need double the quantity, i.e. 450g/1lb tagliatelle for three or four hearty appetites, which takes just 3–4 minutes to cook.

Carbonara Sauce with Spaghetti

AN ALL-TIME FAVOURITE sauce that is
perfect for spaghetti or tagliatelle.
This version has plenty of pancetta
or bacon and is not too creamy, but
you can vary the amounts.

Serves 4

INGREDIENTS

350g/12oz fresh or dried spaghetti

For the carbonara sauce
30ml/2 tbsp olive oil
1 small onion, finely chopped
8 pancetta or lean bacon, cut into
    1cm/¹/₂ in strips
4 eggs
60ml/4 tbsp crème fraîche
60ml/4 tbsp freshly grated Parmesan
    cheese, plus extra to serve
salt and ground black pepper

1 Heat the oil in a frying pan, add the
onion and cook, stirring, over a low
heat, for 5 minutes until softened.

2 Add the strips of pancetta or
bacon to the onion in the pan and
cook for about 10 minutes, stirring
almost all the time.

3 Meanwhile, cook the pasta in a
pan of salted boiling water
according to the instructions on the
packet, until *al dente*.

4 Put the eggs, crème fraîche and
grated Parmesan in a bowl. Grind
in plenty of pepper, then beat the
mixture together well.

5 Drain the pasta, turn it into the pan
with the pancetta or bacon and
toss well to mix.

6 Turn the heat off under the pan.
Immediately add the egg mixture
and toss vigorously so that it cooks
lightly and coats the pasta.

7 Quickly taste for seasoning, then
divide among four warmed bowls
and sprinkle with black pepper. Serve
immediately, with extra grated
Parmesan offered separately.

Clam and Tomato Sauce with Vermicelli

CLAM AND TOMATO SAUCE is a regular dish in Neopolitan restaurants, and is often served with vermicelli or spaghetti. Fresh mussels could be substituted for the clams.

Serves 4

INGREDIENTS
350g/12oz vermicelli

For the clam and tomato sauce
1kg/2¼lb fresh hard-shell clams
250ml/8fl oz/1 cup dry white wine
2 garlic cloves, bruised
1 large handful fresh flat leaf parsley
30ml/2 tbsp olive oil
1 small onion, finely chopped
8 ripe plum tomatoes, peeled, seeded and
*   finely chopped*
½–1 fresh red chilli, seeded and
*   finely chopped*
salt and ground black pepper

1 Scrub the clams thoroughly under cold running water and discard any that are open and that do not close when they are sharply tapped against the work surface.

2 Pour the wine into a large pan, add the garlic cloves and half the parsley, then the clams. Cover tightly with the lid and bring to the boil over a high heat. Cook for about 5 minutes, shaking the pan frequently, until the clams have opened.

3 Tip the clams into a large colander set over a bowl and let the liquid drain through. Set aside the clams until cool enough to handle, then remove about two-thirds of them from their shells, pouring the clam liquid into the bowl of cooking liquid. Discard any clams that have failed to open. Set both shelled and unshelled clams aside, keeping the unshelled clams warm in a bowl covered with a lid.

4 Heat the oil in a pan, add the onion and cook gently, stirring frequently, for about 5 minutes until softened and lightly coloured. Add the tomatoes, then strain in the clam cooking liquid. Add the chilli and salt and pepper to taste. Chop the remaining parsley finely and set aside.

5 Bring to the boil, half-cover the pan and allow to simmer gently for 15–20 minutes.

6 Meanwhile, cook the pasta according to the instructions on the packet, until it is *al dente*.

7 Add the shelled clams to the tomato sauce, stir well and heat through very gently for 2–3 minutes.

8 Drain the cooked pasta well and tip it into a warmed bowl. Taste the sauce for seasoning, then pour the sauce over the pasta and toss everything together well. Serve garnished with the reserved clams and sprinkled with parsley.

Cream and Parmesan Sauce with Spinach and Ricotta Ravioli

THIS CREAMY PARMESAN SAUCE is a perfect accompaniment to home-made spinach and ricotta ravioli but would be just as delicious on store-bought tortelloni or any other fresh pasta with a stuffing to give flavour.

Serves 8

INGREDIENTS

500g/1¼lb fresh pasta dough
grated fresh Parmesan cheese, to serve
salt and ground black pepper

For the filling
45ml/3 tbsp butter
175g/6oz fresh spinach leaves, trimmed,
  washed and shredded
200g/7oz/scant 1 cup ricotta cheese
25g/1oz/⅓ cup freshly grated
  Parmesan cheese
freshly grated nutmeg
1 small (US medium) egg

For the cream and Parmesan sauce
50g/2oz/¼ cup butter
120ml/4fl oz/½ cup double (heavy) cream
50g/2oz/⅔ cup freshly grated
  Parmesan cheese

1 To make the filling, melt the butter in a pan, add the spinach and salt and pepper to taste and cook over a medium heat for about 5 minutes, stirring frequently, until the spinach is wilted and tender. Increase the heat to high. Stir until the water boils off and the spinach is quite dry.

2 Tip the spinach into a bowl and set aside until cold, then add the ricotta, grated Parmesan and freshly grated nutmeg to taste. Beat well to mix, taste for seasoning, then add the egg and beat well again.

3 Using a pasta machine, roll out one-quarter of the pasta into a 90–100cm/36–40in strip. Cut the strip with a sharp knife into two 45–50cm/18–20in lengths (you can do this during rolling if the strip gets too long to manage).

4 Using a teaspoon, put 10–12 little mounds of the filling along one side of one of the pasta strips, spacing them evenly. Brush a little water around each mound, then fold the plain side of the pasta strip over the filling.

5 Starting from the folded edge, press down gently with your finger-tips around each mound of filling, pushing the air out at the unfolded edge. Sprinkle lightly with flour.

6 With a fluted pasta wheel, cut along each long side, then in between each mound to make small square shapes.

7 Put the ravioli on floured dish-towels, sprinkle lightly with flour and allow to dry while repeating the process with the remaining pasta, to give you 80–96 ravioli altogether.

8 Drop the ravioli into a large pan of boiling salted water, bring back to the boil and boil for 4–5 minutes.

9 Meanwhile, make the sauce. Gently heat the butter, cream and Parmesan in a medium pan until the butter and Parmesan have melted.

10 Increase the heat and simmer for a minute or two until the sauce is slightly reduced, then add salt and pepper to taste.

11 Drain the ravioli and divide them equally among eight warmed large bowls. Drizzle the sauce over them and serve sprinkled with Parmesan and ground pepper.

VARIATION

This cheese sauce would also work well with a baked pasta dish such as macaroni. Sprinkle the top generously with grated Parmesan before baking.

Butter and Herb Sauce with Chitarra Spaghetti

YOU CAN USE JUST one favourite herb or several for this recipe. The result is the simplest way to dress up pasta but also one of the tastiest.

Serves 4

INGREDIENTS

400g/14oz fresh or dried spaghetti alla chitarra
freshly grated Parmesan cheese, to serve

For the butter and herb sauce
2 good handfuls mixed fresh herbs, plus extra herb leaves and flowers to garnish
115g/4oz/½ cup butter
salt and ground black pepper

1 Cook the pasta in boiling, lightly salted water according to the packet instructions, until almost *al dente*.

2 To make the sauce, chop the herbs coarsely or finely, as you prefer.

3 When the pasta is almost *al dente*, melt the butter in a large pan. As soon as it sizzles, drain the pasta and add it to the pan, then sprinkle in the herbs with salt and pepper to taste.

4 Toss over a medium heat until the pasta is coated in butter and herbs. Serve immediately in warmed bowls, sprinkled with extra herb leaves and flowers. Pass round some extra grated Parmesan separately.

VARIATION

If you like the flavour of garlic with herbs, add one or two crushed garlic cloves when melting the butter.

Bolognese Sauce with Ravioli

PERHAPS ONE OF THE most famous
pasta sauces outside Italy, Bolognese
sauce is a rich ragoût from the city
of Bologna in Emilia-Romagna, an
area famous for fine foods.

Serves 6

INGREDIENTS

225g/8oz cottage cheese
*30ml/2 tbsp freshly grated Parmesan
    cheese, plus extra for serving*
*1 egg white, beaten, including extra
    for brushing*
1.5ml/¼ tsp ground nutmeg
300g/11oz fresh pasta dough
flour, for dusting
salt and ground black pepper

For the Bolognese sauce

1 medium onion, finely chopped
1 garlic clove, crushed
150ml/¼ pint/⅔ cup beef stock
350g/12oz minced (ground) extra-lean beef
120ml/4fl oz/½ cup red wine
*30ml/2 tbsp concentrated tomato
    purée (paste)*
400g/14oz can chopped plum tomatoes
2.5ml/½ tsp chopped fresh rosemary
1.5ml/¼ tsp ground allspice

1 To make the filling, mix the cottage
cheese, Parmesan, egg white,
seasoning and nutmeg together.

2 Roll the pasta into thin sheets, then
place small amounts of filling along
the pasta in rows, leaving a gap of
5cm/2in between them. Moisten round
the filling with beaten egg white.

3 Place a second sheet of pasta
lightly over the top. Press between
each pocket to remove air, and seal.

4 Cut into rounds with a fluted
ravioli or pastry cutter. Transfer to a
floured dishtowel and leave to rest for
at least 30 minutes before cooking.

5 To make the Bolognese sauce, cook
the onion and garlic in the stock
for 5 minutes or until all the stock has
reduced. Add the beef and cook
quickly to brown, breaking up the meat
with a fork.

VARIATION

*Stir in a handful of chopped chicken
livers with the minced beef to add a
more meaty richness to the sauce.*

6 Add the wine, tomato purée,
chopped tomatoes, rosemary and
allspice. Bring to the boil and simmer
for 1 hour. Season to taste.

7 Cook the ravioli in a large pan
of boiling, salted water for
4–5 minutes. (Cook in batches to
stop them sticking together.) Drain
thoroughly. Serve topped with the
Bolognese sauce. Serve grated
Parmesan cheese separately.

Cream and Walnut Sauce on Pansotti

THIS WALNUT AND CREAM pesto is a simplified version of the one traditionally served with pansotti in Liguria. It would go equally well with any pasta stuffed with ricotta or spinach, or for a less rich alternative serve it with plain pasta shells.

Serves 6–8

INGREDIENTS
500g/1¼lb herb-flavoured pasta dough
with eggs
50g/2oz/¼ cup butter
freshly grated Parmesan cheese, to serve
salt and ground black pepper

For the filling
250g/9oz/generous 1 cup ricotta cheese
115g/4oz/1¼ cups freshly grated
Parmesan cheese
1 large handful fresh basil leaves,
finely chopped
1 large handful fresh flat leaf parsley,
finely chopped
a few sprigs of fresh marjoram or oregano,
leaves removed and finely chopped
1 garlic clove, crushed
1 small (US medium) egg

For the cream and walnut sauce
90g/3½oz/1 cup shelled walnuts
1 garlic clove
60ml/4 tbsp extra virgin olive oil
120ml/4fl oz/½ cup double (heavy) cream

1 To make the filling, put the ricotta cheese, Parmesan cheese, basil, parsley, marjoram or oregano, garlic and egg in a bowl. Season with salt and ground black pepper to taste, and beat well to mix.

2 To make the sauce, put the walnuts, garlic clove and oil in a food processor and process to a paste, adding up to 120ml/4fl oz/½ cup warm water, through the feeder tube, to thin down the paste.

3 Spoon the mixture into a bowl and add the cream. Beat well to mix, then season to taste.

4 Using a pasta machine, roll out one-quarter of the pasta into a 90–100cm/36–40in strip. Cut the strip with a sharp knife into two 45–50cm/ 18–20in lengths (you can do this during rolling if the strip gets too long to manage).

5 Using a 5cm/2in square ravioli cutter, cut eight to ten squares from one of the pasta strips.

6 Using a teaspoon, put a mound of filling in the centre of each square.

7 Brush a little water around the edge of each square, then fold the square diagonally in half over the filling to make a triangle. Press gently to seal.

8 Spread out the pansotti on clean floured dishtowels, sprinkle lightly with flour and set aside to dry, while repeating the process with the remaining dough, to make a total of 64–80 pansotti.

9 Cook the pansotti in a large pan of boiling salted water for 5 minutes.

10 Meanwhile, put the walnut sauce in a large, warmed bowl and add a ladleful of the pasta cooking water to thin it down. Melt the butter in a small pan until sizzling.

11 Drain the pansotti and tip them into the bowl of walnut sauce. Drizzle the butter over them, toss well, then sprinkle with grated Parmesan. Alternatively, toss the pansotti in the melted butter, spoon into warmed individual bowls and drizzle over the sauce. Serve the dish immediately, with extra Parmesan handed round separately.

COOK'S TIP

Take care not to overfill the pansotti, or they will burst open during cooking.

Spinach Sauce with Seafood Pasta Shells

Soft cheese and spinach complements all kinds of pasta. This sauce would be perfect with any filled fresh pasta.

Serves 4

INGREDIENTS

32 large dried pasta shells
salt and ground black pepper

For the filling

15g/½oz/1 tbsp butter or margarine
8 spring onions (scallions), thinly sliced
6 tomatoes
225g/8oz cooked peeled prawns (shrimp)
175g/6oz can white crab meat, drained and flaked

For the spinach sauce

225g/8oz/1 cup soft cheese
90ml/6 tbsp milk
pinch of freshly grated nutmeg
115g/4oz frozen chopped spinach, thawed and drained
salt and ground black pepper

1 Preheat the oven to 150°C/300°F/ Gas 2. Melt the butter or margarine in a pan and cook the spring onions for 3–4 minutes, or until soft.

2 Plunge the tomatoes into boiling water for 1 minute, then into cold water. Slip off the skins. Halve the tomatoes, remove the seeds and cores and roughly chop the flesh.

3 Cook the pasta shells in lightly salted boiling water for about 10 minutes, or until *al dente*. Drain.

4 To make the sauce, put the soft cheese and milk into a pan and heat gently, stirring until blended. Season with salt, ground black pepper and a pinch of nutmeg.

5 Measure 30ml/2 tbsp of cheese mixture into a bowl. Add the onions, tomatoes, prawns, and crab meat. Mix well. Spoon the filling into the shells and place in a single layer in a shallow ovenproof dish. Cover with foil and cook for 10 minutes.

6 Stir the spinach into the remaining sauce. Bring to the boil and simmer gently for 1 minute, stirring constantly. Serve hot, drizzled over pasta.

Smoked Haddock and Parsley Sauce for Pasta

THIS HEARTY SAUCE made with smoked haddock makes any hollow pasta shape into a healthy lunch or supper. Shell-shaped pasta is ideal to hold the sauce, but corkscrew and tube shapes work just as well.

Serves 4

INGREDIENTS

225g/8oz pasta shells
15g/¹/₂oz toasted flaked (sliced) almonds,
*   to serve*

For the smoked haddock and
**   parsley sauce**
450g/1lb smoked haddock fillet
1 small leek or onion, thickly sliced
300ml/¹/₂ pint/1¹/₄ cups milk
bouquet garni
25g/1oz/2 tbsp butter or margarine
25g/1oz/¹/₄ cup plain (all-purpose) flour
30ml/2 tbsp chopped fresh parsley
salt and ground black pepper

1 Remove all the skin and any bones from the haddock and discard. Put the fish into a pan with the leek or onion, milk and bouquet garni. Bring to the boil, cover and simmer gently for 8–10 minutes, or until the fish flakes easily.

2 Strain, reserving the milk for making the sauce, and discard the bouquet garni.

3 Put the butter or margarine, flour and reserved milk into a pan. Bring to the boil and whisk until smooth. Season and add the fish and leek or onion.

4 Cook the pasta in a large pan of boiling salted water until *al dente*. Drain thoroughly and stir into the sauce with the chopped parsley. Serve immediately, sprinkled with toasted flaked almonds.

Prawn and Vodka Sauce with Pasta

THE COMBINATION OF PRAWNS , vodka and pasta may seem unusual, but has become a modern classic in Italy. Here it is served with two-coloured pasta, but the sauce goes equally well with short shapes.

Serves 4

INGREDIENTS
350g/12oz fresh or dried paglia e fieno

For the prawn and vodka sauce
30ml/2 tbsp olive oil
¼ large onion, finely chopped
1 garlic clove, crushed
15–30ml/1–2 tbsp sun-dried tomato paste
200ml/7fl oz/1 cup double (heavy) cream
12 large raw prawns (shrimp), peeled
   and chopped
30ml/2 tbsp vodka
salt and ground black pepper

1 Heat the oil in a medium pan, add the onion and garlic and cook gently, stirring frequently, for about 5 minutes or until softened.

2 Add the tomato paste and stir for 1–2 minutes, then add the cream and bring to the boil, stirring. Season with salt and pepper to taste and let the sauce bubble until it starts to thicken slightly. Remove from the heat.

3 Cook the pasta according to the instructions on the packet, until *al dente*. When it is almost ready, add the prawns and vodka to the sauce; toss over a medium heat for 2–3 minutes, or until the prawns turn pink.

4 Drain the pasta and turn it into a warmed bowl. Pour the sauce over and toss well. Divide among warmed bowls and serve immediately.

COOK'S TIP

This sauce is best served as soon as it is ready, otherwise the prawns will overcook and become tough. Make sure that the pasta has only a minute or two of cooking time left before adding the prawns to the sauce.

Smoked Salmon and Cream Sauce with Penne

THIS MODERN WAY OF serving pasta is popular all over Italy. The three essential ingredients combine beautifully, and the dish is very quick and easy to make.

Serves 4

INGREDIENTS
350g/12oz penne

*For the smoked salmon and
   cream sauce*
115g/4oz thinly sliced smoked salmon
2–3 fresh thyme sprigs
25g/1oz/2 tbsp butter
150ml/¼ pint/⅔ cup double (heavy) cream
salt and ground black pepper

1 Cook the pasta in boiling salted water until it is *al dente*.

2 Meanwhile, using kitchen scissors, cut the smoked salmon into thin strips, about 5mm/¼in wide. Strip the leaves from the thyme sprigs.

3 Melt the butter in a large pan. Stir in the cream with one-quarter of the salmon and thyme leaves, then season with pepper. Heat gently for 3–4 minutes, stirring constantly. Do not allow to boil. Taste for seasoning.

4 Drain the pasta and toss it in the cream and salmon sauce. Divide among four warmed bowls and top with the remaining salmon and thyme leaves. Serve immediately.

VARIATION

Although penne is traditional with this sauce, it also goes very well with fresh ravioli stuffed with spinach and ricotta.

Spicy Sausage Sauce with Tortiglioni

SERVE THIS HEADY PASTA DISH with a robust Sicilian red wine.

Serves 4

INGREDIENTS
300g/11oz dried tortiglioni
salt and ground black pepper

For the spicy sausage sauce
30ml/2 tbsp olive oil
1 onion, finely chopped
1 celery stick, finely chopped
2 large garlic cloves, crushed
1 fresh red chilli, seeded and chopped
450g/1lb ripe plum tomatoes, peeled and
 finely chopped
30ml/2 tbsp tomato purée (paste)
150ml/¼ pint/⅔ cup red wine
5ml/1 tsp sugar
175g/6oz spicy salami, rind removed
30ml/2 tbsp chopped parsley, to garnish
freshly grated Parmesan cheese, to serve

1 Heat the oil in a flameproof casserole or large pan, then add the onion, celery, garlic and chilli. Cook gently, stirring frequently, for about 10 minutes, until softened.

2 Add the tomatoes, tomato purée, wine, sugar and salt and pepper to taste and bring to the boil, stirring. Lower the heat, cover and simmer gently, stirring occasionally, for about 20 minutes. Add a few spoonfuls of water if the sauce becomes too thick.

3 Meanwhile, cook the pasta in a large pan of rapidly boiling, salted water according to the instructions on the packet, until *al dente*.

4 Chop the salami into bitesize chunks and add to the sauce. Heat through, then taste for seasoning.

5 Drain the pasta, tip it into a large bowl, then pour the sauce over and toss to mix. Sprinkle over the parsley and serve with grated Parmesan.

COOK'S TIP

Buy the salami for this dish in one piece so that you can chop it into large chunks.

Wild Mushroom Sauce with Fusilli

A VERY RICH DISH with an earthy flavour and lots of garlic, this makes an ideal main course for vegetarians, especially if it is followed by a crisp green salad.

Serves 4

INGREDIENTS

150g/5oz wild mushrooms preserved in olive oil
30ml/2 tbsp butter
150g/5oz fresh wild mushrooms, sliced if large
5ml/1 tsp finely chopped fresh thyme
5ml/1 tsp finely chopped fresh marjoram or oregano, plus extra herbs to serve
4 garlic cloves, crushed
350g/12oz fresh or dried fusilli
200ml/7fl oz/scant 1 cup double (heavy) cream
salt and ground black pepper

1 Drain about 15ml/1 tbsp of the oil from the mushrooms into a medium pan. Slice the preserved mushrooms into bitesize pieces, if they are large.

2 Add the butter to the oil in the pan and heat over a low heat until sizzling. Add the preserved and the fresh mushrooms, the chopped herbs and the garlic. Season to taste.

SAFETY TIP

Unless you're an expert, or know of one who will identify them for you, it's safer not to pick mushrooms in the wild, but buy them instead from a reliable source.

3 Simmer over a medium heat, stirring frequently, for about 10 minutes or until the fresh mushrooms are soft and tender.

4 Meanwhile, cook the pasta in boiling salted water according to the packet instructions, until *al dente*.

5 As soon as the mushrooms are cooked, increase the heat to high and toss the mixture with a wooden spoon to boil off any excess liquid. Pour in the cream and bring to the boil. Season if necessary.

6 Drain the pasta and turn it into a warmed bowl. Pour the sauce over and toss well. Serve immediately, sprinkled with chopped fresh herbs.

Sauces for Meat Dishes

The simplest, most basic sauce for meat is traditional gravy. Based on the juices from the cooked meat, this is one of the most widely used, everyday sauces. It is on this, together with a basic brown sauce, that many meat sauces are based. But not only brown sauces are used with meat – you'll also find white, creamy sauces and a delicate butter sauce in this section.

Many red meat dishes provide the opportunity for quite robust sauces, using warm spices, garlic or pungent herbs, simmered with red wine or tomato mixtures for added richness. The contrasting flavours of tangy fruits or sweet-and-sour mixtures are particularly successful with rich meats such as beef, lamb, pork, venison or duck, notably the popular combination of venison with cranberries.

Although usually classed as a white meat, pork is also a natural partner for the tangy sweetness of apples or oranges, and pairs well with sweet-and-sour type sauces. More delicately flavoured white meats or poultry, such as veal, chicken and turkey, go well with cream sauces or sauces based on white wine.

Avocado Sauce with Lemon Chicken

THIS GREAT SAUCE IS based on the classic Mexican dip, guacamole. Made without the addition of water, it could be used as a dip with raw vegetables, or even as a sandwich filling. Here it teams perfectly with chicken.

Serves 4

INGREDIENTS
juice of 2 lemons
45ml/3 tbsp olive oil
2 garlic cloves, crushed
5 chicken breast portions, 200g/7oz each
2 beefsteak tomatoes, cored and cut in half
salt and ground black pepper

For the avocado sauce
1 ripe avocado
50ml/2fl oz/¼ cup sour cream
45ml/3 tbsp fresh lemon juice
2.5ml/½ tsp salt
50ml/2fl oz/¼ cup water

To serve
chopped fresh coriander (cilantro), to garnish

1 Combine the lemon juice, oil, garlic, 2.5ml/½ tsp salt, and a little pepper in a bowl. Stir to mix.

2 Arrange the chicken portions in one layer in a shallow glass dish. Pour over the lemon mixture and turn to coat evenly. Cover and allow to stand for at least 1 hour at room temperature, or chill overnight.

3 For the avocado sauce, cut the avocado in half, remove the stone (pit) and scrape the flesh into a food processor or blender.

4 Add the sour cream, lemon juice and salt, and process until smooth. Add the water and process just to blend. If necessary, add more water to thin the sauce. Transfer to a bowl, taste and adjust the seasoning, if necessary. Set aside.

5 Preheat the grill (broiler) to hot. Heat a ridged griddle or heavy frying pan. Remove the chicken from the marinade and pat dry.

6 When the griddle or frying pan is hot, add the chicken and cook, turning often, for about 10 minutes, until they are cooked through.

7 Meanwhile, arrange the tomato halves, cut-sides up, on a baking sheet and season lightly with salt and pepper. Grill (broil) for about 5 minutes, until hot and bubbling.

8 To serve, place a chicken portion, tomato half, and a spoonful of avocado sauce on each plate. Sprinkle with coriander and serve.

VARIATION

To cook the chicken on a barbecue, prepare the fire, and, when the coals are glowing red and covered with grey ash, spread them in a single layer. Set an oiled barbecue grill rack about 13cm/5in above the coals and cook the chicken portions for 15–20 minutes, until lightly charred and cooked through. Allow extra olive oil for basting.

Salsa Picante with Chicken Enchiladas

THIS "HOT" SALSA IS actually a low-heat version using seeded green chillies, and is also cooled down by the sour cream. As well as serving it with enchiladas, it would make a good side dish with kebabs of chicken or pork.

Serves 4

INGREDIENTS

8 wheat tortillas
175g/6oz/1½ cups grated Cheddar cheese
1 onion, finely chopped
350g/12oz cooked chicken, cut into
    small chunks
300ml/½ pint/1¼ cups sour cream
1 avocado, sliced and tossed in lemon juice,
    to garnish

For the salsa picante
1–2 green chillies
15ml/1 tbsp vegetable oil
1 onion, chopped
1 garlic clove, crushed
400g/14oz can chopped tomatoes
30ml/2 tbsp tomato purée (paste)
salt and ground black pepper

1 To make the salsa picante, cut the chillies in half lengthways and carefully remove the cores and seeds. Slice the chillies very finely. Heat the oil in a frying pan and fry the onion and garlic for about 3–4 minutes until softened. Add the tomatoes, tomato purée and chillies. Simmer gently, uncovered, for 12–15 minutes, stirring the mixture frequently.

2 Pour the sauce into a food processor or blender, and process until smooth. Return to the heat and cook very gently, uncovered, for a further 15 minutes. Season to taste then set aside.

3 Preheat the oven to 180°C/350°F/ Gas 4 and butter a shallow ovenproof dish. Take one tortilla and sprinkle with a good pinch of cheese and chopped onion, about 40g/1½oz of the chicken and 15ml/1 tbsp of salsa picante.

4 Pour over 15ml/1 tbsp of sour cream, roll up and place, seam-side down, in the dish. Make seven more enchiladas.

5 Pour the remaining salsa over the top and sprinkle with cheese and onion. Bake for 25–30 minutes until golden. Serve with the remaining cream. Garnish with the sliced avocado.

Marsala Cream Sauce with Turkey

MARSALA MAKES A VERY rich and tasty sauce. The addition of lemon juice gives it a refreshing tang, which helps to offset the richness.

Serves 6

INGREDIENTS

6 turkey breast steaks
45ml/3 tbsp plain (all-purpose) flour
30ml/2 tbsp olive oil
25g/1oz/2 tbsp butter
salt and ground black pepper

For the Marsala cream sauce
175ml/6fl oz/¾ cup dry Marsala
60ml/4 tbsp lemon juice
175ml/6fl oz/¾ cup double (heavy) cream

To serve
lemon wedges and chopped fresh parsley,
  to garnish
mangetouts (snow peas) and green beans

1 Put each turkey steak between two sheets of clear film (plastic wrap) and pound with a rolling pin to flatten. Cut each steak in half or into quarters, discarding any sinew.

2 Spread out the flour in a shallow bowl. Season well with salt and pepper and coat the meat.

3 Heat the oil and butter in a wide, heavy pan until sizzling. Add as many pieces of turkey as you can, and sauté over a medium heat for about 3 minutes on each side until crispy and tender.

4 Transfer to a warmed serving dish with tongs and keep hot. Repeat with the remaining turkey. Lower the heat.

5 To make the sauce, mix the Marsala and lemon juice in a jug (pitcher), add to the oil and butter in the pan and raise the heat. Bring to the boil, stirring in the sediment, then add the cream.

6 Simmer, stirring constantly, until the sauce is reduced and glossy. Taste for seasoning.

7 Spoon the sauce over the turkey, garnish with the lemon wedges and parsley and serve with the vegetables.

COOK'S TIP

To make this sauce without using the pan drippings, omit the oil and heat the butter in a pan before adding the other ingredients.

Walnut and Pomegranate Sauce with Duck Breasts

THIS IS AN EXTREMELY EXOTIC sweet-and-sour sauce, which originally comes from Iran.

Serves 4

INGREDIENTS
4 duck breasts, about 225g/8oz each

For the walnut and pomegranate sauce
30ml/2 tbsp olive oil
2 onions, very thinly sliced
2.5ml/½ tsp ground turmeric
400g/14oz/2⅓ cups walnuts, roughly chopped
1 litre/1¾ pints/4 cups duck or chicken stock
6 pomegranates
30ml/2 tbsp caster (superfine) sugar
60ml/4 tbsp lemon juice
salt and ground black pepper

1 To make the sauce, heat half the oil in a frying pan. Add the onions and turmeric, and cook gently until soft.

2 Transfer to a pan, add the walnuts and stock, then season with salt and pepper. Stir, then bring to the boil and simmer the mixture, uncovered, for 20 minutes.

3 Cut the pomegranates in half and scoop out the seeds. Reserve the seeds of one pomegranate. Transfer the remaining seeds to a blender and process to break them up. Strain through a sieve, to extract the juice, and stir in the sugar and lemon juice.

4 Score the skin of the duck breasts in a diamond pattern with a sharp knife. Heat the remaining oil in a frying pan or griddle and place the duck breasts in it, skin-side down.

5 Cook gently for 10 minutes, pouring off the fat, until the skin is dark golden and crisp. Turn the duck over and cook for a further 3–4 minutes. Transfer to a plate and leave to rest. Deglaze the frying pan with the pomegranate juice, then add the walnut and stock mixture and simmer for 15 minutes until thickened.

6 Slice the duck and serve drizzled with a little sauce, and garnished with the reserved pomegranate seeds. Serve the remaining sauce separately.

Redcurrant Sauce with Lamb Burgers

THE SWEET-SOUR redcurrant sauce is the perfect complement to lamb and would go equally well with grilled or roast lamb steaks.

Serves 4

INGREDIENTS

500g/1¼lb minced (ground) lean lamb
1 small onion, finely chopped
30ml/2 tbsp finely chopped fresh mint
30ml/2 tbsp finely chopped fresh parsley
115g/4oz mozzarella cheese
30ml/2 tbsp oil, for basting
salt and ground black pepper

For the redcurrant sauce
115g/4oz/1 cup fresh or frozen redcurrants
10ml/2 tsp clear honey
5ml/1 tsp balsamic vinegar
30ml/2 tbsp finely chopped mint

1 In a large bowl, mix together the minced lamb, chopped onion, mint and parsley until evenly combined. Season well with plenty of salt and ground black pepper.

2 Roughly divide the meat mixture into eight equal pieces and use your hands to press each of the pieces into flat rounds.

3 Cut the mozzarella into four chunks. Place a chunk of cheese on half the lamb rounds. Top each with another round of meat mixture.

4 Press each of the two rounds of meat together firmly, making four flattish burger shapes. Use your fingers to blend the edges and seal in the cheese completely.

5 To make the sauce, place all the ingredients in a bowl and mash them together with a fork. Season well with salt and ground black pepper.

6 Brush the lamb burgers with olive oil and or grill (broil) for 10 minutes turning once, until golden brown. Serve with the sauce.

VARIATION

To make a quick version of the sauce, melt a jar of ready-made redcurrant sauce with balsamic vinegar and mint.

Tomato Sauce with Greek Lamb Sausages

FOR A QUICK AND EASY tomato sauce, passata can be enlivened with the addition of sugar, bay leaves and onions. The sausages will add more flavour as they simmer in the smooth sauce. As an alternative you could try using turkey instead of lamb.

Serves 4

INGREDIENTS

50g/2oz/1 cup fresh breadcrumbs
150ml/¼ pint/⅔ cup milk
675g/1½lb minced (ground) lamb
30ml/2 tbsp grated onion
3 garlic cloves, crushed
10ml/2 tsp ground cumin
30ml/2 tbsp chopped fresh parsley
flour, for dusting
olive oil, for frying
salt and ground black pepper
fresh flat leaf parsley, to garnish

For the tomato sauce
600ml/1 pint/2½ cups passata (bottled
    strained tomatoes)
5ml/1 tsp sugar
2 bay leaves
1 small onion, peeled

1 Mix together the breadcrumbs and milk. Add the lamb, onion, garlic, cumin and parsley and season well.

2 Shape the mixture into little fat sausages, about 5cm/2in long and roll them in flour.

3 Heat about 60ml/4 tbsp olive oil in a pan. Fry the sausages in the oil for about 8 minutes, turning them until evenly browned. Remove and place on kitchen paper to drain.

4 Put the passata, sugar, bay leaves and whole onion in a pan and simmer for 20 minutes.

5 Add the sausages and cook for 10 minutes more. Serve garnished with parsley.

Pesto with Roast Leg of Lamb

THE INTENSE AROMAS OF fresh basil and garlic combine irresistibly with lamb, and the pine nuts and Parmesan make a delectable crunchy crust during roasting.

Serves 6

INGREDIENTS

2.25–2.75kg/5–6lb leg of lamb

For the pesto

90g/3½oz/1¾ cups fresh basil leaves
4 garlic cloves, coarsely chopped
45ml/3 tbsp pine nuts
150ml/¼ pint/⅔ cup olive oil
50g/2oz/⅔ cup freshly grated Parmesan cheese
5ml/1 tsp salt, or to taste

1 To make the pesto, combine the basil, garlic and pine nuts in a food processor, and process until finely chopped. With the motor running, slowly add the oil in a steady stream. Scrape the mixture into a bowl. Stir in the Parmesan and salt.

2 Set the lamb in an ovenproof dish. Make several slits in the meat with a knife, and spoon pesto into each slit.

3 Coat the surface of the lamb in a thick, even layer of the remaining pesto. Cover the meat and leave to stand for 2 hours at room temperature, or chill overnight. Preheat the oven to 180°C/350°F/Gas 4.

4 Place the lamb in the oven and roast, allowing about 20 minutes per 450g/1lb if you like rare meat, or 25 minutes per 450g/1lb if you prefer it medium-rare. Turn the lamb occasionally during roasting.

5 Remove the leg of lamb from the oven, cover it loosely with foil, and let it rest for about 15 minutes before carving and serving.

VARIATION

Lamb steaks or lamb chops could also be coated with this delicious pesto.

Creamy Calvados and Apple Sauce with Noisettes of Pork

THIS DISH IS IDEAL AS part of a formal menu to impress guests. Buttered gnocchi or griddled polenta and red cabbage are suitable accompaniments.

Serves 4

INGREDIENTS

30ml/2 tbsp plain (all-purpose) flour
4 noisettes of pork, about 175g/6oz each, firmly tied
25g/1oz/2 tbsp butter
4 baby leeks, finely sliced
5ml/1 tsp mustard seeds, coarsely crushed
30ml/2 tbsp Calvados
150ml/¼ pint/⅔ cup dry white wine
2 eating apples, peeled, cored and sliced
150ml/¼ pint/⅔ cup double (heavy) cream
30ml/2 tbsp chopped fresh parsley
salt and ground black pepper

1 Place the flour in a bowl and add plenty of seasoning. Turn the noisettes in the flour mixture to coat them lightly.

2 Melt the butter in a heavy frying pan and cook the noisettes until golden on both sides. Remove from the pan and set aside.

3 Add the leeks to the fat remaining in the pan and cook for 5 minutes. Stir in the mustard seeds and pour in the Calvados, then carefully ignite it to burn off the alcohol.

4 When the flames have died down pour in the wine and replace the pork. Cook gently for 10 minutes, turning the pork frequently.

5 Add the apples and cream and simmer for 5 minutes, or until the apples are tender. Taste for seasoning, then stir in the chopped parsley and serve at once.

Chilli-nectarine Relish with Pork Chops

Pork and fruit are a classic combination, and this spicy nectarine relish is the perfect partner for griddled pork chops.

Serves 4

INGREDIENTS

250ml/8fl oz/1 cup fresh orange juice
45ml/3 tbsp olive oil
2 garlic cloves, minced (ground)
5ml/1 tsp ground cumin
15ml/1 tbsp coarsely ground black pepper
8 pork loin chops, about 2cm/³⁄₄in thick,
    well trimmed
salt

For the chilli-nectarine relish
1 small fresh green chilli pepper
30ml/2 tbsp honey
juice of ¹⁄₂ lemon
250ml/8fl oz/1 cup chicken stock
2 nectarines, pitted and chopped
1 garlic clove, crushed
¹⁄₂ onion, finely chopped
5ml/1 tsp grated fresh root ginger
1.5ml/¹⁄₄ tsp salt
15ml/1 tbsp chopped fresh
    coriander (cilantro)

1 Roast the chilli over a gas flame, holding it with tongs, or under the grill (broiler). Cool for 5 minutes.

2 Wearing rubber gloves, remove the charred skin from the chilli. Discard seeds if a less hot flavour is desired. Finely chop the chilli and place in a pan.

3 Add the honey, lemon juice, chicken stock, nectarines, garlic, onion, ginger and salt. Bring to the boil, then simmer, stirring occasionally, for about 30 minutes. Stir in the coriander and set aside.

4 In a small bowl, combine the orange juice, oil, garlic, cumin and pepper. Stir to mix.

5 Arrange the pork chops, in one layer, in a shallow dish. Pour over the orange juice mixture and turn to coat. Cover and leave to stand for at least one hour, or chill overnight.

6 Remove the pork from the marinade and pat dry with kitchen paper. Season lightly with salt.

7 Heat a frying pan or ridged griddle. Add the meat and cook for 5 minutes, or until browned. Turn and cook on the other side for 10 minutes more. (Work in batches if necessary.) Serve immediately, with the relish.

COOK'S TIP

The relish can be made in advance, then covered and stored in the refrigerator overnight for the flavours to develop.

Sage and Orange Sauce with Pork Fillet

SAGE IS OFTEN PARTNERED with pork –
there seems to be a natural affinity
– and the addition of orange to the
sauce balances the flavour.

Serves 4

INGREDIENTS
2 x 350g/12oz pork fillets (tenderloin)
10ml/2 tsp unsalted (sweet) butter
salt and ground black pepper
orange wedges and sage leaves, to garnish

For the sage and orange sauce
120ml/4fl oz/¹⁄₂ cup dry sherry
175ml/6fl oz/³⁄₄ cup chicken stock
2 garlic cloves, very finely chopped
grated rind and juice of 1 unwaxed orange
3–4 sage leaves, finely chopped
10ml/2 tsp cornflour (cornstarch)

1 Season the pork fillets lightly with
salt and pepper.

2 Melt the butter in a heavy, flame-
proof casserole over a medium-
high heat, then add the meat and cook
for 5 minutes, turning to brown all
sides evenly.

3 Add the sherry, boil for about
1 minute, then add the stock, garlic,
orange rind and chopped sage. Bring to
the boil and reduce the heat to low,
then cover and simmer for 20 minutes,
turning once.

4 Transfer the pork to a warmed
platter and cover to keep warm.

5 Bring the sauce to the boil. Blend
the cornflour and orange juice and
stir into the sauce, then boil gently over
a medium heat for a few minutes,
stirring frequently, until the sauce is
slightly thickened.

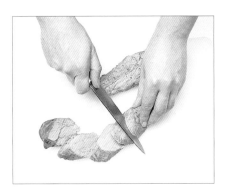

6 Slice the pork diagonally and pour
the meat juices into the sauce.

7 Spoon a little sauce over the pork
and garnish with orange wedges
and sage leaves. Serve the remaining
sauce separately.

COOK'S TIP

• *The meat is cooked if the juices run
clear when the meat is pierced, or when
a meat thermometer inserted into the
thickest part of the meat registers
66°C/150°F.*
• *If fresh sage is not available, try using
rosemary as a substitute, as this also
goes very well with pork.*

Smoked Cheese Sauce with Veal Escalopes

SHEEP'S MILK CHEESE melted with cream makes a simple sauce for serving with pan-fried veal escalopes. The escalopes are used as purchased, not beaten thin.

Serves 4

INGREDIENTS

25g/1oz/2 tbsp butter
15ml/1 tbsp extra virgin olive oil
8 small veal escalopes (scallops)
2 garlic cloves, crushed
250g/9oz/3½ cups button (white) or
   closed-cup mushrooms, sliced
150g/5oz/1¼ cups frozen peas, thawed
60ml/4 tbsp brandy
250ml/8fl oz/1 cup whipping cream
150g/5oz smoked sheep's milk
   cheese, diced
ground black pepper
sprigs of flat leaf parsley, to garnish

1 Melt half the butter with the oil in a large, heavy frying pan. Season the escalopes with plenty of pepper and brown them in batches on each side over a high heat. Reduce the heat and cook for about 5 minutes on each side until just done. The escalopes should feel firm to the touch, with a very light springiness.

2 Lift the escalopes on to a serving dish and keep hot.

3 Add the remaining butter to the pan. When it melts, stir-fry the garlic and mushrooms for about 3 minutes.

4 Add the peas, pour in the brandy and cook until all the pan juices have been absorbed. Season lightly. Using a slotted spoon, remove the mushrooms and peas and place on top of the escalopes. Pour the cream into the pan.

5 Stir in the diced cheese. Heat gently until the cheese has melted. Season with pepper only and pour over the escalopes and vegetables. Serve immediately, garnished with sprigs of flat leaf parsley.

VARIATION

This dish works well with lean pork steaks. Ensure that pork is well cooked, with a slightly longer frying time.

Sweet-and-sour Sauce with Pork

THE COMBINATION OF SWEET-and-sour flavours is popular in Venetian cooking, especially with meat and liver. This recipe is given extra bite with the addition of crushed mixed peppercorns. Served with fresh beans tossed with crispy bacon, it is truly delectable.

Serves 2

INGREDIENTS

1 whole pork fillet (tenderloin), about
   350g/12oz
25ml/1½ tbsp plain (all-purpose) flour
30–45ml/2–3 tbsp olive oil
salt and ground black pepper
broad (fava) beans tossed with grilled
   (broiled) bacon, to serve

For the sweet-and-sour sauce
250ml/8fl oz/1 cup dry white wine
30ml/2 tbsp white wine vinegar
10ml/2 tsp sugar
15ml/1 tbsp mixed peppercorns,
   coarsely ground

1 Cut the pork diagonally into thin slices. Place between two sheets of clear film (plastic wrap) and pound lightly with a rolling pin to flatten.

2 Spread out the flour in a shallow bowl. Season well with salt and pepper and coat the meat.

3 Heat 15ml/1 tbsp of the oil in a wide, heavy pan or frying pan and add as many slices of pork as the pan will hold. Fry over a medium to high heat for 2–3 minutes on each side, or until crispy and tender. Remove with a fish slice (spatula) and set aside. Repeat with the remaining pork, adding more oil as necessary.

4 Mix the wine, wine vinegar and sugar in a jug (pitcher). Pour into the pan and stir vigorously over a high heat until reduced, scraping the pan to incorporate the sediment. Stir in the peppercorns and return the pork to the pan. Spoon the sauce over the pork until it is evenly coated and heated through. Serve with the broad beans tossed with grilled bacon.

COOK'S TIP

Grind the peppercorns in a pepper grinder, or crush them with a mortar and pestle.

Cumberland Sauce with Gammon

THIS SAUCE WAS INVENTED to honour the Duke of Cumberland, who commanded the troops at the last battle on English soil, against the Scots. It can be served hot or cold, with gammon or venison.

Serves 8–10

INGREDIENTS

2.25kg/5lb smoked or unsmoked
  gammon (cured ham) joint
1 onion
1 carrot
1 celery stick
bouquet garni sachet
6 peppercorns

For the glaze
whole cloves
50g/2oz/¼ cup soft light brown or
  demerara (raw) sugar
30ml/2 tbsp golden (light corn) syrup
5ml/1 tsp English (hot) mustard powder

For the Cumberland sauce
juice and shredded rind of 1 orange
30ml/2 tbsp lemon juice
120ml/4fl oz/½ cup port or red wine
60ml/4 tbsp redcurrant jelly

1 Soak the gammon overnight in a cool place in plenty of cold water to cover. Discard this water. Put the joint into a large pan and cover it again with more cold water. Bring the water to the boil slowly and skim any scum from the surface with a slotted spoon.

2 Add the vegetables and seasonings, cover and simmer very gently for 2 hours. (The meat can also be cooked in the oven at 180°C/350°F/ Gas 4. Allow 30 minutes per 450g/1lb.)

3 Leave the meat to cool in the liquid for 30 minutes. Then remove it from the liquid and strip off the skin neatly with the help of a knife (use rubber gloves if the gammon is too hot to handle).

4 Score the fat in diamonds with a sharp knife and stick a clove in the centre of each diamond. Preheat the oven to 180°C/350°F/Gas 4.

5 Put the sugar, syrup and mustard powder in a small pan and heat gently to melt them. Place the gammon in a roasting pan and spoon over the glaze. Bake it for about 20 minutes, or until golden brown, then put it under a hot grill (broiler) to colour.

6 Allow the meat to stand in a warm place for 15 minutes before carving (this makes carving much easier and tenderizes the meat).

7 For the Cumberland sauce, put the orange and lemon juice into a pan with the port or wine and redcurrant jelly, and heat gently to melt the jelly. Pour boiling water on to the orange rind, strain, and add the rind to the sauce. Cook gently for two minutes. Serve the sauce hot.

COOK'S TIP

Gammon is often not as strongly salted as it once was, so it may not be necessary to soak overnight before cooking to remove the salty flavour.

Cranberry Sauce with Venison

VENISON STEAKS ARE NOW readily available. Lean and low in fat, they make a healthy choice for a special occasion. Served with a sauce of fresh seasonal cranberries, port and ginger, they make a dish with a wonderful combination of flavours.

Serves 4

INGREDIENTS

30ml/2 tbsp sunflower oil

4 venison steaks

2 shallots, finely chopped

salt and ground black pepper

fresh thyme sprigs, to garnish

creamy mashed potatoes and broccoli,
    to serve

For the cranberry sauce

1 orange

1 lemon

75g/3oz/¾ cup fresh or frozen cranberries

5ml/1 tsp grated fresh root ginger

1 fresh thyme sprig

5ml/1 tsp Dijon mustard

60ml/4 tbsp redcurrant jelly

150ml/¼ pint/⅔ cup ruby port

1 For the sauce, pare the rind thinly from half the orange and half the lemon using a vegetable peeler, then cut into very fine strips.

2 Blanch the strips in a small pan of boiling water for about 5 minutes until tender. Strain the strips and refresh under cold water.

3 Squeeze the juice from the orange and lemon and then pour into a small pan. Add the fresh or frozen cranberries, ginger, thyme sprig, mustard, redcurrant jelly and port. Cook the sauce mixture over a low heat until the jelly melts.

4 Bring the sauce to the boil, stirring occasionally, then cover the pan and reduce the heat. Cook gently, for about 15 minutes, or until the cranberries are just tender.

5 Heat the oil in a heavy frying pan, add the venison steaks and cook over a high heat for 2–3 minutes.

6 Turn over the steaks and add the shallots to the pan. Cook the steaks on the other side for 2–3 minutes, depending on whether you like rare or medium cooked meat.

7 Just before the end of cooking, pour in the sauce and add the strips of orange and lemon rind. Leave the sauce to bubble for a few seconds to thicken slightly, then remove the thyme sprig and adjust the seasoning to taste.

8 Transfer the venison steaks to warmed plates and spoon over the sauce. Garnish with thyme sprigs and serve accompanied by creamy mashed potatoes and broccoli.

COOK'S TIP

When frying venison, always remember the briefer the better; venison will turn to leather if subjected to fierce heat after it has reached the medium-rare stage. If you dislike any hint of pink, cook it to this stage then let it rest in a low oven for a few minutes.

VARIATION

When fresh cranberries are unavailable, use redcurrants instead. Stir them into the sauce towards the end of cooking with the orange and lemon rinds.

Black Bean Sauce with Beef and Broccoli Stir-fry

THIS CHINESE BEEF DISH is a quick stir-fry with a richly flavoured marinade that bubbles down into a luscious, dark sauce.

Serves 4

INGREDIENTS

225g/8oz lean fillet or rump (round) steak
15ml/1 tbsp sunflower oil
225g/8oz broccoli
115g/4oz baby corn, diagonally halved
45–60ml/3–4 tbsp water
2 leeks, diagonally sliced
225g/8oz can water chestnuts, sliced

For the marinade

15ml/1 tbsp fermented black beans
30ml/2 tbsp dark soy sauce
30ml/2 tbsp Chinese rice vinegar or (hard) cider vinegar
15ml/1 tbsp sunflower oil
5ml/1 tsp sugar
2 garlic cloves, crushed
2.5cm/1in piece of fresh root ginger, peeled and finely chopped

1 To make the marinade, mash the fermented black beans in a non-metallic bowl. Add the remaining ingredients and stir well.

2 Cut the steak into thin slices across the grain, then add them to the marinade. Stir the steak well to coat it in the marinade. Cover the bowl and leave for several hours.

3 Heat the oil in a frying pan. Drain the steak (reserving the marinade). When the oil is hot, add the meat and stir-fry for 3–4 minutes. Transfer to a plate and set aside.

4 Cut the broccoli into small florets. Reheat the oil in the pan, add the broccoli, corn and water. Cover and steam gently for 5 minutes.

5 Add the leeks and water chestnuts to the broccoli mixture and toss over the heat for 1–2 minutes. Return the meat to the pan, pour over the reserved marinade and toss briefly over a high heat before serving.

COOK'S TIP

Fermented black beans are cooked, salted and fermented whole soya beans; they are available from Asian stores.

Roquefort and Walnut Butter with Rump Steak

MAKE A ROLL OF this savoury cheese butter to keep in the refrigerator, ready to top plain steaks or chops.

Serves 4

INGREDIENTS

15ml/1 tbsp finely chopped fresh chives
15ml/1 tbsp olive oil or sunflower oil
4 x 130g/4½ oz lean rump (round) steaks
120ml/4fl oz/½ cup dry white wine
30ml/2 tbsp crème fraîche
salt and ground black pepper
fresh chives, to garnish

For the Roquefort and walnut butter
2 shallots, chopped
75g/3oz/6 tbsp butter, slightly softened
150g/5oz Roquefort cheese
30ml/2 tbsp finely chopped walnuts

1 Sauté the shallots in one-third of the butter. Tip into a bowl and add half the remaining butter, the cheese, walnuts, chopped chives and pepper to taste. Chill lightly, roll in foil to a sausage shape and chill again until firm.

2 Heat the remaining butter with the oil and cook the steaks to your liking. Season and remove from the pan.

3 Pour the wine into the pan and stir to incorporate any sediment. Bubble up the liquid for a minute or two, then stir in the crème fraîche. Season with salt and pepper and pour over the steaks.

4 Cut pats of the Roquefort butter from the roll and put one on top of each steak. Garnish with chives and serve. Green beans make an ideal accompaniment to this dish.

COOK'S TIP

The butter can also be stored in the freezer, but it is easier to cut it into rounds before freezing, so you can remove just as many as you need, without thawing the rest.

Sauces for Fish Dishes

You might expect all sauces for fish to be very delicate and light in flavour, but that's not always the case. Certainly in this chapter you'll find a classic white parsley sauce: the perfect partner for white fish or fishcakes. But you'll also discover some more surprising combinations – a tangy orange and caper sauce to pep up plain white fish, and a chilli barbecue sauce to serve with salmon steaks.

There are some flavours that are natural partners for fish, such as lemon or dill, which can be used in classic white or white wine sauces, or in butters to serve with whole fish, fillets or steaks. Some of the classic pairings that have become enduring favourites cannot be ignored. The rich, oily flesh of mackerel balances perfectly with the tangy acidity of a gooseberry sauce, and the slightly sharp flavour of sorrel offsets the richness of salmon and transforms it into a sophisticated dinner-party dish.

As with any sauce, there are no hard-and-fast rules, but the general guideline is that white fish pairs best with subtle cream sauces and herb butters, whereas oily fish can take more robust flavours, such as spices or tangy fruits.

Orange and Caper Sauce with Skate

A WONDERFULLY SWEET-SOUR, creamy sauce to add zest to otherwise plain white fish.

Serves 4

INGREDIENTS
4 skate wings, about 200g/7oz each
25g/1oz/2 tbsp butter
350ml/12fl oz/1½ cups fish stock

For the orange and caper sauce
25g/1oz/2 tbsp butter
1 onion, chopped
fish bones and trimmings
5ml/1 tsp black peppercorns
300ml/½ pint/1¼ cups dry white wine
2 small oranges
15ml/1 tbsp capers, drained
60ml/4 tbsp crème fraîche
salt and ground white pepper

1 To make the sauce, melt the butter and add the onion. Sauté over a moderate heat until the onion is lightly browned.

2 To the sauce, add the fish bones and trimmings and peppercorns, then pour in the wine. Cover and simmer gently for 30 minutes.

3 Using a serrated knife, peel the oranges, ensuring all the white pith is removed. Ease the segments away from the membrane.

4 Place the skate in a frying pan, add the butter and the fish stock and poach for 10–15 minutes, depending on thickness.

5 Strain the wine mixture into a clean pan. Add the capers and orange segments together with any juice, and heat through. Lower the heat and gently stir in the crème fraîche and seasoning. Serve the skate wings and the sauce, garnished with parsley.

VARIATION

For an unusual change, try using ruby grapefruit instead of the orange – this goes particularly well with oily fish such as trout or tuna.

Parsley Sauce with Haddock

ONE OF THE MOST classic sauces for fish is parsley sauce – a perfect partner for any white fish.

Serves 4

INGREDIENTS

4 haddock fillets, about 175g/6oz each
25g/1oz/2 tbsp butter
150ml/¼ pint/⅔ cup milk
150ml/¼ pint/⅔ cup fish stock
1 bay leaf
salt and ground black pepper

For the parsley sauce
25g/1oz/2 tbsp butter
20ml/4 tsp plain (all-purpose) flour
60ml/4 tbsp single (light) cream
1 egg yolk
45ml/3 tbsp chopped fresh parsley
grated rind and juice of ½ lemon

1 Place the fish in a frying pan, add the butter, milk, fish stock, bay leaf and seasoning, and heat to simmering point.

2 Lower the heat, cover the pan and poach the fish for 10–15 minutes, depending on the thickness of the fillets, until the fish is tender and the flesh begins to flake. Transfer to a warm serving plate, cover and keep warm.

3 Make the sauce. Return the cooking liquid to the heat and bring to the boil, stirring. Simmer for about 4 minutes, then remove and discard the bay leaf.

4 Melt the butter in a pan, stir in the flour and cook, stirring constantly, for 1 minute.

5 Remove the pan from the heat and gradually stir in the fish cooking liquid.

6 Return to the heat and bring to the boil, stirring. Simmer for about 4 minutes, stirring frequently. Remove the pan from the heat.

7 In a bowl, blend the cream into the egg yolk, then stir this into the sauce with the parsley.

8 Reheat gently, stirring, for a few minutes; do not allow to boil.

9 Remove from the heat and add the lemon juice and rind, and season to taste. Pour into a warmed sauceboat and serve with the fish.

Vermouth and Chèvre Sauce with Pan-fried Cod

A SMOOTH SAUCE OF vermouth and light, creamy chèvre teams deliciously with chunky, white cod.

Serves 4

INGREDIENTS

4 cod fillets, about 150g/5oz each, skinned
15ml/1 tbsp olive oil
salt and ground black pepper
fresh flat leaf parsley, to garnish

For the vermouth and chèvre sauce

15ml/1 tbsp olive oil
4 spring onions (scallions), chopped
150ml/¼ pint/⅔ cup dry vermouth,
    preferably Noilly Prat
300ml/½ pint/1¼ cups fish stock
45ml/3 tbsp crème fraîche
65g/2½oz chèvre (goat's cheese),
    rind removed, and chopped
30ml/2 tbsp chopped fresh parsley
15ml/1 tbsp chopped fresh chervil

1 Remove any stray bones from the cod fillets. Rinse the fish under cold running water and pat dry with kitchen paper. Place the pieces on a plate and season generously.

VARIATION

Instead of cod you could use salmon, haddock or plaice. The cooking time may change according to the thickness of the fish fillets.

2 Heat a non-stick frying pan, then add the oil, swirling it around to coat the base. Add the pieces of cod and cook, without turning or moving them, for 4 minutes, or until nicely caramelized.

3 Turn each piece over and cook the other side for a further 3 minutes, or until just firm. Remove them to a serving plate and keep hot.

4 To make the sauce, heat the oil in a frying pan and stir-fry the spring onions for 1 minute. Add the vermouth and cook until reduced by half. Add the stock and cook again until reduced by half. Stir in the crème fraîche and chèvre and simmer for about 3 minutes.

5 Add salt and pepper to taste, stir in the herbs and spoon over the fish. Garnish with parsley.

Dill and Mustard Sauce with Sole

THIS SAUCE WILL GIVE A TANGY, Scandinavian flavour that is perfect with fish. Sole is used here but the dill and mustard would combine with virtually any fish.

Serves 3–4

INGREDIENTS

3–4 lemon sole fillets
melted butter, for brushing
salt and ground black pepper
lemon slices and dill sprigs, to garnish

For the dill and mustard sauce
25g/1oz/2 tbsp butter
20g/³⁄₄oz/3 tbsp plain (all-purpose) flour
300ml/¹⁄₂ pint/1¹⁄₄ cups hot fish stock
15ml/1 tbsp white wine vinegar
45ml/3 tbsp chopped fresh dill
15ml/1 tbsp wholegrain mustard
10ml/2 tsp sugar
2 egg yolks

1 Preheat the grill (broiler) to medium-high. Brush the fish with melted butter, season on both sides and cut two or three slashes in the flesh. Grill (broil) for 4 minutes, then transfer to a warmed place and keep warm while you make the sauce.

2 Melt the butter over a medium heat and stir in the flour. Cook for 1–2 minutes over a low heat, stirring constantly to remove any lumps.

3 Remove from the heat and gradually blend in the hot stock. Return to the heat, bring to the boil, stirring constantly, then simmer for 2–3 minutes.

VARIATION

A fennel and mustard sauce could also be made using chopped fennel leaves instead of the dill. Replace the wholegrain mustard with Dijon.

4 Remove the pan from the heat and beat in the white wine vinegar, dill, mustard and sugar.

5 Using a fork, beat the yolks in a small bowl and gradually add a small quantity of hot sauce. Return to the pan, whisking vigorously. Continue whisking over a very low heat for a further minute. Serve immediately with the grilled sole, garnished with lemon slices and dill sprigs.

Gooseberry Sauce with Mackerel

GOOSEBERRIES AND MACKEREL ARE a classic combination; the tart sauce offsets the rich, oily fish.

Serves 4

INGREDIENTS

4 fresh mackerel, about 350g/12oz each, cleaned
salt and ground black pepper

For the gooseberry sauce
15g/½oz/1 tbsp butter
225g/8oz gooseberries, trimmed
1 egg, beaten
pinch of ground mace or ginger, or a few drops of orange flower water (optional)
fresh flat leaf parsley, to garnish

1 Melt the butter in a pan, add the gooseberries, then cover and cook over a low heat, shaking the pan until the gooseberries are just tender.

2 Meanwhile, preheat the grill (broiler). Season the fish inside and out with salt and black pepper.

3 Cut two or three slashes in the skin on both sides of each mackerel, then grill (broil) for 15–20 minutes, or until cooked, turning once.

4 Purée the gooseberries with the egg in a food processor or blender, or mash the gooseberries thoroughly in a bowl with the egg. Press the gooseberry mixture through a sieve.

5 Return the gooseberry mixture to the pan and reheat gently, stirring, but do not allow to boil. Add the mace, ginger or orange flower water, if using, and season to taste. Serve the sauce hot with the mackerel, garnished with fresh parsley.

COOK'S TIPS

• *For the best flavour, look for triple strength orange flower water, which can be obtained from chemists (drugstores) and good food stores.*
• *If fresh gooseberries are not in season, canned ones make an alternative. Make sure they do not contain added sugar or the tart flavour will not be achieved.*

Herb Sauce with Sardines

THE ONLY ESSENTIAL ACCOMPANIMENT to this luscious herb sauce is fresh, crusty bread to mop up the tasty juices. The sauce is also quite delicious served with plain chicken breast portions. For the best flavour, cook the sardines on a barbecue.

Serves 4

INGREDIENTS

12–16 fresh sardines
oil, for brushing
juice of 1 lemon
crusty bread, to serve

For the herb sauce
15ml/1 tbsp butter
4 spring onions (scallions), chopped
1 garlic clove, finely chopped
grated rind of 1 lemon
30ml/2 tbsp finely chopped fresh parsley
30ml/2 tbsp finely chopped fresh chives
30ml/2 tbsp finely chopped fresh basil
30ml/2 tbsp green olive paste
10ml/2 tsp balsamic vinegar
salt and ground black pepper

3 Add the lemon rind and remaining sauce ingredients to the onions and garlic in the pan and keep warm on the edge of the hob (stovetop) or barbecue, stirring occasionally. Do not allow the mixture to boil.

4 Brush the sardines lightly with oil and sprinkle with lemon juice, salt and pepper. Cook on a barbecue (grill) for about 2 minutes on each side, over a medium heat. Serve with the warm sauce and fresh crusty bread.

1 To clean the sardines, use a pair of small kitchen scissors to slit the fish along the belly and pull out the innards. Wipe the fish with kitchen paper and then arrange on a wire rack.

2 To make the sauce, melt the butter in a small pan and gently sauté the spring onions and garlic for about 2 minutes, shaking the pan occasionally, until softened but not browned.

Orange Butter Sauce with Sea Bream

THIS RICH BUTTER SAUCE, sharpened with tangy orange juice, goes well with the firm white flesh of sea bream.

Serves 2

INGREDIENTS
2 sea bream or porgy, about 350g/12oz
   each, scaled and gutted
10ml/2 tsp Dijon mustard
5ml/1 tsp fennel seeds
30ml/2 tbsp olive oil
225g/8oz mixed salad leaves

For the orange butter sauce
30ml/2 tbsp frozen orange
   juice concentrate
175g/6oz/¾ cup unsalted (sweet)
   butter, diced
salt and cayenne pepper

1 Slash the fish four times on each side. Combine the mustard and fennel seeds, then spread over both sides of the fish.

2 Brush each side of the fish with olive oil and grill (broil) under a preheated grill (broiler) for 10–12 minutes, turning the fish once midway through the cooking time.

3 Place the orange juice concentrate in a bowl and heat over a pan of simmering water. Remove the pan from the heat and gradually whisk in the butter until creamy. Season well.

4 Dress the salad leaves with the remaining olive oil, and arrange with the fish on two plates. Spoon the sauce over the fish and serve.

COOK'S TIP

Alternatively, cook the fish on a medium-hot barbecue. This is much easier if you use a hinged wire rack that holds the fish firmly and enables you to turn the fish without it breaking up.

Tahini Sauce with Baked Fish

THIS NORTH AFRICAN RECIPE evokes all the colour and rich flavours of Mediterranean cuisine, and the tahini sauce makes an unusual combination of tastes.

Serves 4

INGREDIENTS

1 whole fish, about 1.2kg/2½lb, scaled
  and cleaned
10ml/2 tsp coriander seeds
4 garlic cloves, sliced
10ml/2 tsp harissa sauce
90ml/6 tbsp olive oil
6 plum tomatoes, sliced
1 mild onion, sliced
3 preserved lemons or 1 fresh lemon
plenty of fresh herbs, such as bay leaves,
  thyme and rosemary
salt and ground black pepper
extra herbs, to garnish

For the tahini sauce
75ml/2½fl oz/⅓ cup light tahini
juice of 1 lemon
1 garlic clove, crushed
45ml/3 tbsp finely chopped fresh parsley
  or coriander (cilantro)

1 Preheat the oven to 200°C/400°F/ Gas 6. Grease the base and sides of a large, shallow ovenproof dish.

2 Slash the fish diagonally on both sides with a sharp knife. Finely crush the coriander seeds and garlic with a mortar and pestle. Mix with the harissa sauce and about 60ml/4 tbsp of the olive oil.

3 Spread a little of the harissa, coriander and garlic paste inside the cavity of the fish. Spread the remainder over each side of the fish and set aside.

4 Sprinkle the tomatoes, onion and preserved or quartered fresh lemon into the dish. Sprinkle with the remaining oil, and season. Put the fish on top. Tuck plenty of herbs around it.

5 Bake the fish, uncovered, for about 25 minutes, or until it has turned opaque – test by piercing the thickest part with a knife.

6 Meanwhile, to make the sauce, put the tahini, lemon juice, garlic and parsley or coriander in a small pan with 120ml/4fl oz/½ cup cold water, and add a little salt and ground black pepper to season. Cook gently until smooth and heated through. Garnish the fish with the herbs, and serve the sauce separately.

COOK'S TIP

If you can't get a suitable large fish, use small whole fish such as red mullet, red snapper or even cod or haddock steaks. Reduce the cooking time slightly.

Tomato Coulis with Marinated Monkfish

A LIGHT BUT WELL-FLAVOURED sauce, this should be made when Italian plum tomatoes are at their ripest. The lime and herb marinade is offset by the sweet tomatoes in the coulis. Serve this delicious dish with a glass of chilled white wine.

Serves 4

INGREDIENTS

30ml/2 tbsp olive oil
finely grated rind and juice of 1 lime
30ml/2 tbsp chopped fresh mixed herbs
5ml/1 tsp Dijon mustard
4 skinless, boneless monkfish fillets
salt and ground black pepper
fresh herb sprigs, to garnish

For the tomato coulis

4 plum tomatoes, peeled and chopped
1 garlic clove, chopped
15ml/1 tbsp olive oil
15ml/1 tbsp tomato purée (paste)
30ml/2 tbsp chopped fresh oregano
5ml/1 tsp soft light brown sugar

1 Place the oil, lime rind and juice, herbs, mustard, and salt and pepper in a small bowl or jug and whisk together until thoroughly mixed.

2 Place the monkfish fillets in a shallow, non-metallic container and pour the lime mixture over. Turn the fish several times in the marinade to coat it. Cover and chill in the refrigerator for 1–2 hours.

3 Meanwhile, make the tomato coulis. Place all the coulis ingredients in a food processor or blender and process until smooth. Season to taste, then cover and chill until required.

4 Preheat the oven to 180°C/350°F/ Gas 4. Using a fish slice (spatula), place each fish fillet on a sheet of greaseproof (waxed) paper big enough to hold it in a parcel.

5 Spoon a little marinade over each piece of fish. Gather the paper loosely over the fish and fold over the edges to secure the parcel tightly. Place on a baking sheet.

6 Bake for 20–30 minutes, or until the fish fillets are cooked, tender and just beginning to flake.

7 Carefully unwrap the parcels and serve the fish fillets immediately with a little of the chilled coulis served alongside, and garnished with a few fresh herb sprigs.

COOK'S TIP

The coulis can be served hot, if you prefer. Simply make as directed in the recipe and heat gently in a pan until almost boiling, just before serving.

Sorrel Sauce with Salmon Steaks

THE SHARP FLAVOUR OF the sorrel sauce balances the richness of the fish. The young plant has the mildest flavour, so try to buy the herb in its spring season when it is at its best.

Serves 2

INGREDIENTS
2 salmon steaks, about 250g/9oz each
5ml/1 tsp olive oil
salt and ground black pepper
fresh sage, to garnish

For the sorrel sauce
15g/¹/₂oz/1 tbsp butter
2 shallots, finely chopped
45ml/3 tbsp crème fraîche
90g/3¹/₂oz fresh sorrel leaves, washed and patted dry

1 Season the salmon steaks with salt and pepper. Brush a non-stick frying pan with the oil.

2 Make the sauce. In a small pan, melt the butter over a medium heat. Add the shallots and fry for 3 minutes, stirring frequently, until just softened.

3 Add the crème fraîche and the sorrel leaves to the shallots and cook until the sorrel is completely wilted, stirring constantly.

4 Meanwhile, place the frying pan over a medium heat until hot. Add the salmon steaks and cook for about 5 minutes, turning once, until the flesh is opaque next to the bone. If you're not sure, pierce the flesh with the tip of a sharp knife; the fish should flake easily.

5 Arrange the salmon steaks on two warmed plates, garnish with sage and serve with the sorrel sauce.

COOK'S TIP

If preferred, cook the salmon steaks in the microwave for 4–5 minutes, in a tightly covered dish, or according to the manufacturer's guidelines.

VARIATION

If sorrel is not available, use finely chopped watercress instead.

Chilli Barbecue Sauce with Salmon

THIS SPICY TOMATO AND mustard sauce is delicious served with chargrilled salmon fillets, especially if you cook them on a barbecue.

Serves 4

INGREDIENTS
4 salmon fillets, about 175g/6oz

For the chilli barbecue sauce
10ml/2 tsp butter
1 small red onion, finely chopped
1 garlic clove, finely chopped
6 plum tomatoes, diced
45ml/3 tbsp tomato ketchup
30ml/2 tbsp Dijon mustard
30ml/2 tbsp dark brown sugar
15ml/1 tbsp clear honey
5ml/1 tsp ground cayenne pepper
15ml/1 tbsp ancho chilli powder
15ml/1 tbsp ground paprika
15ml/1 tbsp Worcestershire sauce

1 To make the barbecue sauce, melt the butter in a large, heavy pan and cook the chopped onion and garlic over a low heat until they are tender and translucent.

2 Stir in the tomatoes and simmer for 15 minutes, stirring occasionally (to break up the tomato pieces).

3 Add the remaining sauce ingredients and simmer for a further 20 minutes.

4 Process the mixture until smooth, in a food processor fitted with a metal blade. Leave to cool.

5 Brush the salmon with the sauce and chill for at least 2 hours. Barbecue (grill) or grill (broil) for about 2–3 minutes on each side, brushing on the sauce when necessary. Serve drizzled with the remaining sauce.

Butter Sauce with Salmon Cakes

THE LEMONY BUTTER SAUCE keeps the salmon fishcakes deliciously moist; they make a real treat for supper or a leisurely breakfast at the weekend.

Makes 6

INGREDIENTS
225g/8oz tail piece of salmon, cooked
30ml/2 tbsp chopped fresh parsley
2 spring onions (scallions), chopped
225g/8oz/2⅔ cups firm mashed potato
I egg, beaten
50g/2oz/I cup fresh white breadcrumbs
butter and oil, for frying (optional)
salt and ground black pepper

For the butter sauce
75g/3oz/6 tbsp butter
grated rind and juice of ½ lemon

I Remove all the skin and bones from the fish and mash or flake it well. Add the chopped parsley, onions and 5ml/ I tsp of the lemon rind (from the sauce ingredients) and season with salt and black pepper.

2 Gently work in the potato and then shape into six rounds.

3 Chill the fishcakes for 20 minutes to allow them to firm up. Coat each fishcake well in egg and then the breadcrumbs. Grill (broil) gently for 5 minutes each side, or until golden, or fry in butter and oil over a medium-hot heat.

4 To make the butter sauce, in a pan, melt the butter over a gentle heat, then whisk in the remaining lemon rind and the lemon juice, together with 15–30ml/I–2 tbsp cold water. Season with salt and ground black pepper to taste. Simmer the sauce for a few minutes and then serve immediately with the fishcakes.

VARIATION

If you like, use a lime instead of the half lemon for a change of flavour. This butter sauce is a quick and easy accompaniment to virtually any fish.

COOK'S TIP

Tail pieces of salmon fillet are usually a good buy and do not contain bones, but any cut of salmon can be used for this dish, so look out for any that are on special offer.

Warm Green Tartare Sauce with Shellfish

A COLOURFUL SAUCE THAT'S good with all kinds of fish and shellfish, particularly fresh scallops, and it looks stunning over black pasta.

Serves 4

INGREDIENTS

350g/12oz black tagliatelle
12 large scallops
60ml/4 tbsp white wine
150ml/¼ pint/⅔ cup fish stock
lime wedges and parsley sprigs, to garnish

For the warm green tartare sauce
120ml/4fl oz/½ cup crème fraîche
10ml/2 tsp wholegrain mustard
2 garlic cloves, crushed
30–45ml/2–3 tbsp fresh lime juice
60ml/4 tbsp chopped fresh parsley
30ml/2 tbsp chopped chives
salt and ground black pepper

4 Put the white wine and fish stock into a pan. Heat to simmering point. Add the scallops and cook very gently for 3–4 minutes (no longer or they will become tough).

5 Remove the scallops from the pan. Boil the wine and stock to reduce by about half and add the tartare sauce to the pan. Heat gently to warm the sauce.

6 Replace the scallops and cook for 1 minute. Spoon over the pasta. Garnish with lime wedges and parsley.

COOK'S TIPS

• *If you are removing the scallops from the shells yourself, remember to wash them first in plenty of cold water.*
• *If the scallops are frozen, thaw them before cooking, as they will probably have been glazed with water and will need to be drained well.*

VARIATIONS

• *This sauce could be made equally well with fresh mussels.*
• *Instead of serving over pasta, this sauce would go particularly well with fish, such as monkfish, which has a flavour reminiscent of lobster.*

1 To make the tartare sauce, blend the crème fraîche, mustard, garlic, lime juice, parsley, chives and seasoning together in a food processor or blender.

2 Cook the pasta in a large pan of boiling, salted water according to the instructions on the packet until *al dente*. Drain thoroughly.

3 Meanwhile, slice the scallops in half, horizontally. Keep any corals whole.

Five-spice and Black Bean Sauce with Stir-fried Squid

THE SPICY ASIAN SAUCE is the ideal accompaniment for stir-fried squid and is very easy to make. It is important to have all the ingredients ready before you start to cook. The squid must be cooked very quickly or it will toughen.

Serves 6

INGREDIENTS

450g/1lb small squid, cleaned
45ml/3 tbsp oil

For the five-spice and black bean sauce

2.5cm/1in piece fresh root ginger, grated
1 garlic clove, crushed
8 spring onions (scallions), cut diagonally into 2.5cm/1in lengths
1 red (bell) pepper, seeded and sliced
1 fresh green chilli, seeded and thinly sliced
6 chestnut mushrooms, sliced
5ml/1 tsp five-spice powder
30ml/2 tbsp black bean sauce
30ml/2 tbsp soy sauce
5ml/1 tsp sugar
15ml/1 tbsp rice wine or dry sherry

1 Rinse the squid and pull away the outer skin. Dry on kitchen paper. Slit the squid open and score the outside into diamonds with a sharp knife. Cut the squid into strips.

2 Heat a wok and add the oil. When it is hot, stir-fry the squid quickly. Remove the squid strips from the wok with a slotted spoon and set aside.

3 For the sauce, add the ginger, garlic, spring onions, red pepper, chilli and mushrooms to the oil remaining in the wok and stir-fry for 2 minutes.

4 Return the squid to the wok and stir in the five-spice powder. Stir in the black bean sauce, soy sauce, sugar and rice wine or sherry. Bring to the boil and cook, stirring, for 1 minute. Serve immediately.

Tartare Sauce with Crab Cakes

WHEN SERVING ANY FRIED fish, tartare sauce is the traditional accompaniment, but it is also delicious with vegetables. Maryland is renowned for its shellfish, and these little crab cakes hail from there.

Serves 4

INGREDIENTS

675g/1½ lb fresh white crab meat
1 egg, beaten
30ml/2 tbsp mayonnaise
15ml/1 tbsp Worcestershire sauce
15ml/1 tbsp sherry
30ml/2 tbsp finely chopped fresh parsley
15ml/1 tbsp finely chopped fresh chives
45ml/3 tbsp olive oil
salt and ground black pepper

For the tartare sauce

1 egg yolk
15ml/1 tbsp white wine vinegar
30ml/2 tbsp Dijon-style mustard
250ml/8fl oz/1 cup vegetable oil
30ml/2 tbsp fresh lemon juice
45ml/3 tbsp finely chopped spring
  onions (scallions)
30ml/2 tbsp chopped drained capers
45ml/3 tbsp finely chopped sour dill pickles
45ml/3 tbsp finely chopped fresh parsley

1 Pick over the crab meat, removing any shell or cartilage. Keep the pieces of crab as large as possible.

2 In a bowl, combine the beaten egg with the mayonnaise, Worcestershire sauce, sherry and herbs. Season to taste. Gently fold in the crab meat.

3 Divide the mixture into eight portions and gently form each into an oval cake.

4 Place on a baking sheet between layers of greaseproof (waxed) paper and chill for at least 1 hour.

5 To make the sauce, in a bowl, beat the egg yolk with a wire whisk. Add the vinegar, mustard, and seasoning, and whisk for about 10 seconds. Whisk in the oil in a slow, steady stream.

6 Add the lemon juice, spring onions, capers, sour dill pickles and parsley and mix well. Check the seasoning. Cover and chill.

7 Preheat the grill (broiler). Brush the crab cakes with the olive oil. Place on an oiled baking sheet, in one layer. Grill (broil) 15cm/6in from the heat until golden brown, about 5 minutes on each side. Alternatively, fry the crab cakes over a medium heat for a few minutes on each side. Serve the crab cakes hot with the tartare sauce.

COOK'S TIPS

For easier handling and to make the crab meat go further, add 50g/2oz/1 cup fresh breadcrumbs and 1 more egg to the crab mixture. Divide the mixture into 12 cakes to serve six. Use dill instead of chives if you prefer.

Sauces for Vegetarian Dishes

Vegetable dishes have until recently been considered the poor-relation among other areas of cooking, but it is not only vegetarians that are becoming more interested in making vegetable dishes more appetizing and interesting. Everyone who is interested in healthy eating is including more vegetable-based meals in their diet.

Vegetables are one of the most versatile of all ingredients. They can provide hearty, cold-weather meals, such as baked marrow (large zucchini) and parsley sauce, and the family favourite, Cheddar cheese sauce with cauliflower. For summer steam fresh vegetables, and serve as a warm vegetable salad with peanut sauce.

The sauces in this chapter, however, are not intended to be served exclusively with vegetable meals. They provide flavour and texture that can be teamed with freshly cooked pasta, such as the green vegetable sauce, or polenta, as in the wild mushroom sauce. Others provide a piquant taste to add flavour to a plainer dish, like the citrus sauce, which adds spice to liven up courgettes (zucchini) or potatoes, but would be equally at home with fish or meat dishes. Any of these sauces will enhance and complement a variety of dishes – whether the flavours are similar or contrasting – if you choose carefully.

Green Vegetable Sauce

This sauce is a medley of cooked fresh vegetables. Tossed with pasta, it's ideal for a fresh, light lunch or supper dish.

Serves 4

INGREDIENTS
450g/1lb dried pasta shapes

For the green vegetable sauce
25g/1oz/2 tbsp butter
45ml/3 tbsp extra virgin olive oil
1 small leek, thinly sliced
2 carrots, diced
2.5ml/¹/₂ tsp sugar
1 courgette (zucchini), diced
75g/3oz/generous ¹/₂ cup green beans
115g/4oz/1 cup frozen peas
1 handful fresh flat leaf parsley, chopped
2 ripe plum tomatoes, peeled and diced
salt and ground black pepper
fried parsley sprigs, to garnish

1 Melt the butter and oil in a medium frying pan. When the mixture sizzles, add the prepared leek and carrots. Sprinkle the sugar over the vegetables and fry over a medium heat, stirring the mixture frequently, for about 5 minutes.

2 Stir the courgette, beans and peas into the sauce, and season with plenty of salt and pepper. Cover and cook over a low to medium heat for 5–8 minutes, or until the vegetables are tender, stirring occasionally.

3 Meanwhile, cook the pasta according to the instructions on the packet.

4 Stir the parsley and chopped tomatoes into the sauce.

5 Serve the sauce immediately, tossed with freshly cooked pasta and garnished with parsley sprigs.

Citrus Sauce with Baby Courgettes

THIS PIQUANT SAUCE IS a refreshing change served with steamed green vegetables, or it would make a tasty dip with roast potato wedges.

Serves 4

INGREDIENTS

350g/12oz baby courgettes (zucchini)

For the citrus sauce

4 spring onions (scallions), finely sliced
2.5cm/1in piece fresh root ginger, grated
30ml/2 tbsp (hard) cider vinegar
15ml/1 tbsp light soy sauce
5ml/1 tsp soft light brown sugar
45ml/3 tbsp vegetable stock
finely grated rind and juice of ½ lemon
    and ½ orange
5ml/1 tsp cornflour (cornstarch)

3 Blend the cornflour with 10ml/2 tsp cold water and add to the sauce. Bring the sauce to the boil, stirring constantly, until thickened.

4 Pour the sauce over the courgettes and gently heat, shaking the pan to coat evenly. Transfer to a warmed serving dish and serve.

VARIATION

Try this sauce with a mixture of baby vegetables, such as courgettes, carrots, turnips, baby corn, patty pan squash etc.

1 Cook the courgettes in lightly salted, boiling water for 3–4 minutes, or until just tender. Drain well.

2 Meanwhile, make the sauce. Put all the sauce ingredients, except the cornflour, into a small pan and bring to the boil. Simmer for 3 minutes.

Peanut Sauce with Warm Vegetable Salad

THIS SPICY SAUCE IS based on the classic Indonesian sauce served with satay, but is equally delicious served with this main-course salad which mixes steamed and raw vegetables. It would also partner vegetable kebabs cooked on a barbecue.

Serves 2–4

INGREDIENTS

8 new potatoes
225g/8oz broccoli, cut into small florets
200g/7oz/1⅓ cups fine green beans
2 carrots, cut into thin ribbons with a
    vegetable peeler
1 red (bell) pepper, seeded and sliced
50g/2oz sprouted beans
salad leaves, to garnish

For the peanut sauce
15ml/1 tbsp sunflower oil
1 bird's eye chilli, seeded and sliced
1 garlic clove, crushed
5ml/1 tsp ground coriander
5ml/1 tsp ground cumin
60ml/4 tbsp crunchy peanut butter
75ml/5 tbsp water
15ml/1 tbsp dark soy sauce
1cm/½ in piece fresh root ginger,
    finely grated
5ml/1 tsp soft dark brown sugar
15ml/1 tbsp lime juice
60ml/4 tbsp coconut milk

1 First make the peanut sauce. Heat the oil in a pan, add the chilli and garlic, and cook for 1 minute, or until softened. Add the spices and cook for a further 1 minute.

2 Stir in the peanut butter and water, then cook for 2 minutes, or until combined, stirring constantly.

3 Add the soy sauce, ginger, sugar, lime juice and coconut milk, then cook over a low heat until smooth and heated through, stirring frequently. Transfer to a bowl.

4 Bring a pan of lightly salted water to the boil, add the potatoes and cook for 10–15 minutes, or until tender. Drain, then halve or thickly slice the potatoes, depending on their size.

5 Meanwhile, steam the broccoli and green beans for 4–5 minutes, or until tender but still crisp. Add the carrots 2 minutes before the end of the cooking time.

6 Arrange the cooked vegetables on a serving platter with the red pepper and sprouted beans. Garnish with salad leaves and serve with the peanut sauce.

COOK'S TIP

Adjust the dipping consistency by adding slightly less water than recommended; you can always stir in a little more at the last minute. Serve the sauce either warm or cold.

Parsley Sauce and Baked Marrow

THIS IS A REALLY glorious way with a simple and modest vegetable. Try to find a small, firm and unblemished specimen for this recipe, as the flavour will be sweet, fresh and delicate. Young marrows do not need peeling.

Serves 4

INGREDIENTS

1 small young marrow (large zucchini), about 900g/2lb
30ml/2 tbsp olive oil
15g/½oz/1 tbsp butter
1 onion, chopped
15ml/1 tbsp plain (all-purpose) flour
300ml/½ pint/1¼ cups milk and single (light) cream, mixed
30ml/2 tbsp chopped fresh parsley
salt and ground black pepper

1 Preheat the oven to 180°C/350°F/ Gas 4. Cut the marrow into pieces measuring about 5 x 2.5cm/2 x 1in.

2 Heat the oil and butter in a flame-proof casserole and fry the onion over a gentle heat until very soft.

3 Add the marrow and sauté for 1–2 minutes and then stir in the flour. Cook for a few minutes.

4 Stir the milk and cream into the vegetable mixture.

5 Add the parsley and seasoning, and stir well.

6 Cover and cook in the oven for 30–35 minutes. If liked, uncover for the final five minutes of cooking to brown the top. Alternatively, serve the marrow in its rich, pale sauce.

VARIATION

Chopped fresh basil or a mixture of basil and chervil also tastes good in this dish.

Roasted Pepper Sauce with Malfatti

A SMOKY PEPPER AND tomato sauce adds the finishing touch to spinach and ricotta dumplings. The Italians call these malfatti – badly made – because of their odd shape.

Serves 4

INGREDIENTS

500g/1¼lb young leaf spinach
1 onion, finely chopped
1 garlic clove, crushed
15ml/1 tbsp extra virgin olive oil
350g/12 oz/1½ cups ricotta cheese
3 eggs, beaten
50g/2oz/scant 1 cup undyed
    dried breadcrumbs
50g/2oz/½ cup plain (all-purpose) flour
50g/2 oz/⅔ cup freshly grated
    Parmesan cheese
freshly grated nutmeg
25g/1oz/2 tbsp butter, melted

For the roasted pepper sauce

2 red (bell) peppers, seeded and quartered
30ml/2 tbsp extra virgin olive oil
1 onion, chopped
400g/14oz can chopped tomatoes
150ml/¼ pint/⅔ cup water
salt and ground black pepper

1 Make the sauce. Preheat the grill (broiler) and grill (broil) the pepper quarters skin-side up until they blister and blacken. Cool slightly, then peel off the skins and chop the flesh.

2 Heat the oil in a pan and lightly sauté the onion and peppers for 5 minutes.

3 Add the tomatoes and water, with salt and pepper to taste. Bring to the boil, lower the heat and simmer gently for 15 minutes.

4 Purée the mixture in a food processor or blender, in batches if necessary, then return to the clean pan and set aside.

5 Trim any thick stalks from the spinach, wash it well if necessary, then blanch in a pan of boiling water for about 1 minute. Drain, refresh under cold water and drain again. Squeeze dry, then chop finely.

6 Put the finely chopped onion, garlic, olive oil, ricotta, eggs and breadcrumbs in a bowl. Add the spinach and mix well. Stir in the flour and 5ml/1 tsp salt with half the Parmesan, then season to taste with pepper and nutmeg.

7 Roll the mixture into 16 small logs and chill lightly.

8 Bring a large pan of water to the boil. Drop in the malfatti in batches and cook them for 5 minutes. Remove with a fish slice (spatula) and toss with the melted butter.

9 To serve, reheat the sauce and divide it among four plates. Arrange four malfatti on each and sprinkle the remaining Parmesan over. Serve immediately.

Quick Tomato Sauce with Baked Cheese Polenta

THIS QUICK TOMATO SAUCE can be prepared from pantry ingredients. The rich flavour of the sauce enhances baked polenta.

Serves 4

INGREDIENTS

5ml/1 tsp salt
250g/9oz/2¼ cups quick-cook polenta
5ml/1 tsp paprika
2.5ml/½ tsp ground nutmeg
75g/3oz/¾ cup grated Gruyère cheese

For the quick tomato sauce

30ml/2 tbsp olive oil
1 large onion, finely chopped
2 garlic cloves, crushed
2 x 400g/14oz cans chopped tomatoes
15ml/1 tbsp tomato purée (paste)
5ml/1 tsp sugar
salt and ground black pepper

1 Preheat the oven to 200°C/400°F/ Gas 6. Line a 28 x 18cm/11 x 7in baking tin (pan) with clear film (plastic wrap). Bring 1 litre/1¾ pints/4 cups water to the boil with the salt.

2 Pour in the quick-cook polenta in a steady stream and cook, stirring constantly, for 5 minutes. Beat in the paprika and nutmeg, then pour into the prepared tin and smooth the surface. Leave to cool.

3 To make the quick tomato sauce, heat the oil in a pan and cook the onion and garlic until soft. Add the chopped tomatoes, tomato purée and sugar. Season, and simmer for 20 minutes.

4 Turn out the polenta on to a board, and cut into 5cm/2in squares. Place half the squares in a greased ovenproof dish. Spoon over half the tomato sauce, and sprinkle with half the cheese. Repeat the layers. Bake for 25 minutes.

Fresh Tomato and Ginger Sauce with Tofu and Potato Rösti

IN THIS RECIPE, the tofu is marinated in a mixture of tamari, honey and oil, flavoured with garlic and ginger. This marinade is then added to the fresh tomatoes to make a thick, creamy tomato sauce with a delicious tang, and the method ensures that the tofu absorbs the same flavours.

Serves 4

INGREDIENTS

425g/15oz tofu, cut into 1cm/½in cubes
4 large potatoes, about 900g/2lb total
   weight, peeled
sunflower oil, for frying
salt and ground black pepper
30ml/2 tsp sesame seeds, toasted

For the fresh tomato and ginger sauce
30ml/2 tbsp tamari or dark soy sauce
15ml/1 tbsp clear honey
2 garlic cloves, crushed
4cm/1½in piece fresh root ginger, grated
5ml/1 tsp toasted sesame oil
15ml/1 tbsp olive oil
8 tomatoes, halved, seeded and chopped

1 For the sauce, mix together the tamari or dark soy sauce, clear honey, garlic, root ginger and toasted sesame oil in a shallow dish.

2 Add the tofu, then spoon the liquid over the tofu and leave to marinate in the refrigerator for at least 1 hour. Turn the tofu occasionally to allow the flavours to infuse (steep).

3 To make the rösti, par-boil the potatoes for 10–15 minutes until almost tender. Leave to cool, then grate coarsely. Season well with salt and freshly ground black pepper. Preheat the oven to 200°C/400°F/Gas 6.

4 Using a slotted spoon, remove the tofu from the marinade and reserve the marinade on one side. Spread out the tofu on a baking tray and bake for 20 minutes, turning occasionally, until golden and crisp on all sides.

5 Take one-quarter of the potato mixture in your hands at a time and form into rough cakes.

6 Heat a frying pan with just enough oil to cover the base. Place the cakes in the frying pan and flatten the mixture, using your hands or a spatula to form rounds about 1cm/½in thick.

7 Cook for about 6 minutes, or until golden and crisp underneath. Carefully turn the rösti over and cook for a further 6 minutes, or until golden brown in colour.

8 Meanwhile, complete the sauce. Heat the oil in a pan, add the reserved marinade and then the tomatoes and cook for 2 minutes, stirring constantly.

9 Reduce the heat and simmer, covered, for 10 minutes, stirring occasionally, until the tomatoes break down. Press the mixture through a sieve to make a thick, smooth sauce.

10 To serve, place a rösti on each of four warm serving plates. Arrange the tofu on top, spoon over the tomato sauce and sprinkle with sesame seeds.

COOK'S TIPS

• *Tamari is a thick, mellow-flavoured Japanese soy sauce, which is sold in Japanese food stores and some larger health-food stores.*
• *Tofu can be rather bland so allow it to marinate for 2–3 hours if possible, to ensure that it is full of flavour.*

Cheddar Cheese Sauce with Cauliflower

SELECT A MATURE FARMHOUSE Cheddar to give this popular dish a full flavour, and season with plenty of ground black pepper.

Serves 4

INGREDIENTS

1.2kg/2½ lb cauliflower florets
   (about 1 large head)
3 bay leaves

For the Cheddar cheese sauce
45ml/3 tbsp butter
45ml/3 tbsp plain (all-purpose) flour
450ml/¾ pint/scant 2 cups milk
50g/2oz/3 cups grated mature (sharp)
   Cheddar cheese
salt and ground black pepper

1 Preheat the oven to 180°C/350°F/ Gas 4. Grease a 30cm/12in round ovenproof dish.

2 Bring a large pan of lightly salted water to a boil. Add the cauliflower florets and cook for 7–8 minutes, or until just tender but still firm. Drain well.

3 To make the sauce, melt the butter in a heavy pan. Whisk in the flour until blended with the butter. Cook until smooth and bubbling, stirring constantly.

4 Gradually add the milk. Bring to a boil and continue cooking, stirring constantly, until the sauce is thickened and smooth.

5 Remove from the heat and stir in the cheese. Season the sauce to taste with salt and pepper.

6 Place the bay leaves on the bottom of the prepared dish. Arrange the cauliflower florets on top in an even layer. Pour the cheese sauce evenly over the cauliflower.

7 Bake for 20–25 minutes, or until golden brown and bubbling. Serve immediately.

VARIATION

You might like to try this with broccoli in place of cauliflower, or with a mixture of the two for a colourful change.

Wild Mushroom Sauce with Polenta and Gorgonzola

THE FLAVOUR OF WILD mushrooms combines well with mascarpone in this sauce to heighten the taste of the polenta. It also makes a delicious topping for baked potatoes.

Serves 4–6

INGREDIENTS
900ml/1½ pints/3¾ cups milk
900ml/1½ pints/3¾ cups water
5ml/1 tsp salt
300g/11oz/2¾ cups polenta
50g/2oz/¼ cup butter
115g/4oz Gorgonzola cheese
fresh thyme sprigs, to garnish

For the wild mushroom sauce
40g/1½ oz/scant 1 cup dried
    porcini mushrooms
150ml/¼ pint/⅔ cup hot water
25g/1oz/2 tbsp butter
115g/4oz/1½ cups button (white)
    mushrooms, chopped
60ml/4 tbsp dry white wine
generous pinch of dried thyme
60ml/4 tbsp mascarpone cheese
salt and ground black pepper

1 Pour the milk and water into a large, heavy pan. Add the salt and bring to the boil. Using a long-handled spoon, stir the liquid briskly with one hand while drizzling in the polenta with the other. When the mixture is thick and smooth, lower the heat to a gentle simmer and cook for about 20 minutes, stirring occasionally.

2 Remove from the heat and stir in the butter and Gorgonzola. Spoon the polenta mixture into a shallow dish and level the surface.

3 Let the polenta set until solid, then cut into wedges.

4 Meanwhile, make the sauce. Soak the porcini in the hot water for 15 minutes. Drain, reserving the liquid. Finely chop the porcini and strain the soaking liquid through a sieve lined with kitchen paper. Discard the kitchen paper.

5 Melt half the butter in a small pan. Sauté the chopped fresh mushrooms for about 5 minutes.

6 Add the wine, porcini and strained soaking liquid, with the dried thyme. Season to taste. Cook for 2 minutes more. Stir in the mascarpone and simmer for a few minutes, until reduced by one-third. Set aside to cool.

7 Heat a ridged griddle pan or grill (broiler), and cook the polenta until crisp. Brush with melted butter, garnish and serve hot with the sauce.

COOK'S TIP

If fresh porcini mushrooms are available, use instead of dried and do not soak. You will need about 175g/6oz fresh porcini for this recipe. They are also sold under the name ceps.

Sauces for Sweet Dishes

Hot and cold sweet sauces can transform a simple scoop of ice cream or a piece of fruit into a complete dessert. A good range of sweet sauces can increase your range of desserts three or four times over. Whether it's a tangy fruit coulis, a rich chocolate sauce, foaming sabayon or creamy custard, you can mix and match your favourite puddings and desserts with sauces to create a new dish every time.

Try a generous drizzle of chocolate sauce over profiteroles for a perfectly indulgent treat, then next time spoon it over your favourite vanilla ice cream. Or, for a lighter, less calorie-laden treat, how about maple yogurt sauce with poached pears, then perhaps serve the maple yogurt sauce with fresh strawberries for another occasion?

It's worth making the most of fruits in season to make deliciously fresh fruit coulis, to use in creative combinations at any time of year. Grilled (broiled) pineapple is irresistible with a luscious spoonful of papaya sauce, or try passion fruit coulis spooned on to scoops of frozen yogurt.

For a more traditional partnership, try dreamy toffee sauce poured on to hot date puddings or old-fashioned castle puddings with real custard.

Papaya Dip with Fresh Fruit

SWEET AND SMOOTH PAPAYA teams up well with crème fraîche to make a luscious, tropical sweet dip which is very good with biscuits or fresh fruit for dipping. If fresh coconut is not available, buy coconut strands and lightly toast them in a hot oven until golden.

Serves 6

INGREDIENTS

2 ripe papayas
200ml/7fl oz/scant 1 cup crème fraîche
1 piece stem (crystallized) ginger
fresh coconut, to decorate
papaya or other fresh fruit, to serve

1 Halve the papayas lengthways, then scoop out and discard the seeds.

2 Scoop out the flesh and process it until smooth in a food processor or blender.

3 Stir in the crème fraîche and process until well blended. Finely chop the ginger and stir it in, then chill until ready to serve.

4 Pierce a hole in the "eye" of the coconut and drain off the liquid. Put the coconut in a plastic bag. Hold it securely in one hand and hit it sharply with a hammer.

5 Remove the shell from a piece of coconut, then snap the nut into pieces no wider than 2.5cm/1in.

6 Use a swivel-bladed vegetable peeler to shave off 2cm/¾in lengths of coconut. Sprinkle these over the dip. Serve with pieces of extra papaya or other fresh fruit.

Malted Chocolate and Banana Dip with Fresh Fruit

CHOCOLATE AND BANANA combine irresistibly in this rich dip, served with fresh fruit in season. For a creamier dip, stir in some lightly whipped cream just before serving.

Serves 4

INGREDIENTS

50g/2oz plain (semisweet) chocolate
2 large ripe bananas
15ml/1 tbsp malt extract (essence)
mixed fresh fruit, such as strawberries,
*   peaches and kiwi fruit, halved or sliced,*
*   to serve*

1 Break the chocolate into pieces and place in a small, heatproof bowl. Stand the bowl over a pan of gently simmering water and stir the chocolate occasionally until it melts. Allow to cool slightly.

2 Break the bananas into pieces and process in a food processor or blender until finely chopped.

3 With the motor running, pour in the malt extract, and continue processing the mixture until it is thick and frothy.

4 Drizzle in the chocolate in a steady stream and process until well blended. Serve immediately, with the prepared fruit alongside.

COOK'S TIP

This smooth dip can be prepared in advance and chilled.

Passion Fruit Coulis with Yogurt Sundaes

FROZEN YOGURT makes a refreshing change from ice cream. Here, it is partnered with a delicious fresh fruit coulis that is simple to make. Some varieties of strawberry may need a little sugar to sweeten them.

Serves 4

INGREDIENTS

175g/6oz/1¹/₂ cups strawberries, hulled and halved

2 peaches, stoned (pitted) and chopped

8 scoops (about 350g/12 oz) vanilla or strawberry frozen yogurt

For the passion fruit coulis

175g/6oz/1¹/₂ cups strawberries, hulled and halved

1 passion fruit

10ml/2 tsp icing (confectioners') sugar (optional)

1 To make the coulis, purée the strawberries. Scoop out the passion fruit pulp and add it to the coulis. Sweeten with icing sugar if necessary.

2 Spoon half the remaining strawberries and half the chopped peaches into four tall sundae glasses.

3 Add a scoop of frozen yogurt. Set aside a few choice pieces of fruit for decoration, and use the rest to make a further layer on the top of each sundae. Top each with a final scoop of frozen yogurt.

4 Pour the passion fruit coulis over, and decorate the sundaes with the reserved strawberries and pieces of peach. Serve immediately.

Hazelnut Dip with Fruit Fondue

FRESH FRUIT IS ALWAYS a good choice for a colourful, simple dessert, and this recipe makes it complete, with a delicious sauce for dipping. Any fruit which can be served raw can be used for this dish. Try to use fruits in a range of different colours for an attractive presentation.

Serves 2

INGREDIENTS

selection of fresh fruits, such as satsumas, kiwi fruit, grapes, physalis and whole strawberries

For the hazelnut dip

50g/2oz/¹/₄ cup soft (farmer's) cheese

150ml/¹/₄ pint/²/₃ cup hazelnut yogurt

5ml/1 tsp vanilla essence (extract)

5ml/1 tsp caster (superfine) sugar

50g/2oz/¹/₃ cup shelled hazelnuts, chopped

1 First prepare the fruits. Peel and segment the satsumas. Then peel the kiwi fruit and cut into wedges. Wash the grapes and peel back the papery casing on the physalis.

2 To make the dip, beat the soft cheese with the hazelnut yogurt, vanilla essence and sugar in a bowl. Stir in three-quarters of the hazelnuts.

3 Spoon into a glass serving dish set on a platter or into small pots on individual plates and sprinkle the remaining hazelnuts on top. Arrange the prepared fruits around the dip and serve immediately.

Lemon and Lime Sauce with Pancakes

THIS IS A TANGY, refreshing sauce and is a perfect foil for the pancakes.

Serves 4

INGREDIENTS

90g/3½oz/ 1 cup plain (all-purpose) flour
pinch of salt
1 egg
300ml/½ pint/1¼ cups milk
vegetable oil, for frying
lemon balm or mint, to decorate

For the lemon and lime sauce

1 lemon
2 limes
50g/2oz/¼ cup caster (superfine) sugar
25ml/1½ tbsp arrowroot
300ml/½ pint/1¼ cups water

1 First, make the sauce. Using a citrus zester, peel the rinds thinly from the lemon and limes taking care not to cut into the pith. Squeeze the juice from the fruit. Place the rind in a pan, cover with water and bring to the boil.

2 Drain through a sieve and reserve the rind.

3 In a small bowl, mix a little sugar with the arrowroot. Blend in enough water to give a smooth paste. Heat the remaining water, pour in the arrowroot mixture, and stir constantly until the sauce boils and thickens. Stir in the remaining sugar, citrus juice and reserved rind. Keep the sauce hot while you make the pancakes.

4 Sift the dry ingredients into a bowl and make a well in the centre. Add the egg and beat in with a wooden spoon. Beat in the milk, drawing in the flour to make a smooth batter.

5 Heat a little oil in a large, heavy frying pan. When hot, pour in a thin layer of batter and cook for 1–2 minutes, or until set. Toss the pancake and cook the other side until golden brown. Transfer the pancake to a plate and keep it warm while you make the rest of the pancakes.

6 Serve with the hot sauce and decorate with lemon balm or mint.

Butterscotch Sauce with Waffles

THIS IS A DELICIOUSLY sweet sauce
which will be loved by everyone.

Serves 4–6

INGREDIENTS
1 pack ready-made waffles
vanilla ice cream, to serve

For the butterscotch sauce
75g/3oz/6 tbsp butter
175g/6oz/³⁄₄ cup dark muscovado
(molasses) sugar
175ml/6fl oz/³⁄₄ cup evaporated milk
50g/2oz/¹⁄₃ cup hazelnuts

1 Warm the waffles in a preheated
oven, according to the instructions
on the packet.

2 Meanwhile, melt the butter and
sugar in a pan, bring to the boil and
boil for 2 minutes. Allow to cool for
5 minutes.

3 Heat the evaporated milk to just
below boiling point, then gradually
stir into the sugar mixture. Cook over a
low heat for 2 minutes, stirring the
sauce frequently.

4 Spread the hazelnuts on a baking
sheet and toast under a hot grill
(broiler) until golden brown. Tip on to
a clean dishtowel and rub briskly to
remove the skins.

5 Chop the nuts roughly and stir
into the sauce. Serve the sauce
hot, poured over scoops of vanilla
ice cream and the warm waffles.

VARIATION

Substitute any nut for the hazelnuts. Pecans,
for example, add a luxurious flavour. You
could also add plump, juicy raisins and
a dash of rum instead of the nuts.

Maple and Cointreau Syrup with Oranges

THE MAPLE SYRUP MAKES this one of the most delicious ways to eat an orange. For an alcohol-free version, simply omit the Cointreau or Grand Marnier.

Serves 4

INGREDIENTS
melted butter, for brushing
4 medium oranges
crème fraîche, to serve

For the maple and Cointreau syrup
30ml/2 tbsp maple syrup
*30ml/2 tbsp Cointreau or Grand
    Marnier liqueur*
20ml/4 tsp butter

1 Preheat the oven to 200°C/400°F/ Gas 6. Cut four double-thickness squares of baking foil, large enough to wrap each of the oranges. Brush the centre of each square of foil with plenty of melted butter.

2 Remove some shreds of orange rind, to decorate. Blanch these, dry them and set them aside.

3 Peel all of the oranges, removing all the white pith and catching the juice in a bowl.

4 Slice each of the oranges crossways into thick slices. Reassemble the slices and place each stack on a square of double thickness baking foil.

5 Tuck the baking foil up securely around the reassembled oranges to keep them in shape, leaving the foil parcels open at the top.

6 To make the syrup, mix together the reserved orange juice, maple syrup and liqueur and spoon the mixture over the oranges.

7 Add a knob (pat) of butter to each parcel and close the foil at the top to seal in the juices. Place the parcels in the oven for 10–12 minutes, or until hot. (The parcels can also be cooked on a hot barbecue, if liked.) Serve with crème fraîche, topped with the reserved shreds of orange rind.

Hot Plum Sauce with Floating Islands

THE PLUM SAUCE CAN be made in advance, then reheated just before you cook the meringues. This makes an unusual, and healthy dessert that is simpler to make than it looks.

Serves 4

INGREDIENTS

2 egg whites
30ml/2 tbsp concentrated apple juice syrup
freshly grated nutmeg

For the hot plum sauce
450g/1lb red plums
300ml/½ pint/1¼ cups apple juice

1 To make the plum sauce, halve the plums and remove the stones (pits). Place them in a wide pan, with the apple juice.

2 Bring to the boil and then cover with a lid and leave to simmer gently for 15–20 minutes, or until the plums are tender.

3 Meanwhile, place the egg whites in a clean, dry bowl and whisk them until they hold soft peaks.

4 Gradually whisk in the apple juice syrup, whisking until the meringue holds fairly firm peaks.

5 Using a tablespoon, scoop the meringue mixture into the gently simmering plum sauce. You may need to cook the "islands" in two batches.

6 Cover and allow to simmer gently for 2–3 minutes, or until the meringues are just set.

7 Serve the dessert straight away, sprinkled with a little freshly grated nutmeg.

Real Custard with Castle Puddings

THIS TRADITIONAL PUDDING is served with one of the most time-honoured sweet sauces – vanilla custard.

Serves 4

INGREDIENTS
about 45ml/3 tbsp berry jam
115g/4oz/½ cup butter
115g/4oz/½ cup caster (superfine) sugar
2 eggs, beaten
few drops of vanilla essence (extract)
130g/4½oz/generous 1 cup self-raising (self-rising) flour

For the real custard
4 eggs
25–30ml/1½–2 tbsp sugar
450ml/¾ pint/scant 2 cups milk
few drops of vanilla essence (extract)

1 Preheat the oven to 180°C/350°F/ Gas 4. Butter four dariole moulds. Put about 10ml/2 tsp jam in the base of each mould.

2 Beat the butter and sugar together until light and fluffy, then gradually beat in the eggs, beating well after each addition and adding the vanilla essence towards the end.

3 Lightly fold in the flour, then divide the mixture among the moulds.

4 Bake the puddings in the oven for about 20 minutes until well risen and a light golden colour.

5 Meanwhile, make the custard. Whisk the eggs and sugar together. Bring the milk to the boil in a heavy pan, preferably non-stick, then slowly pour on to the sweetened egg mixture, stirring constantly.

6 Return the milk and egg mixture to the pan and heat very gently, stirring, until the mixture thickens enough to coat the back of a spoon; do not allow to boil. Stir in the vanilla essence. Cover the pan and remove from the heat.

7 Remove the moulds from the oven, leave to stand for a few minutes, then turn the puddings on to warmed plates and serve with the hot custard.

COOK'S TIPS

• If you prefer, instead of baking the puddings, you can cover and steam them for 30–40 minutes.
• If you do not have dariole moulds, use ramekin dishes.
• Make sure you buy real vanilla essence and not the artificial flavouring. You will only need a drop or two.

Toffee Sauce with Hot Date Puddings

THIS TOFFEE SAUCE IS a great standby for hot or cold desserts. It is equally delicious served with poached apples or drizzled over a steamed pudding.

Serves 6

INGREDIENTS

50g/2oz/¼ cup butter, softened
75g/3oz/6 tbsp light muscovado
   (brown) sugar
2 eggs, beaten
115g/4oz/1 cup self-raising (self-rising) flour
2.5ml/½ tsp bicarbonate of soda
   (baking soda)
175g/6oz/generous 1 cup fresh dates,
   peeled, stoned (pitted) and chopped
75ml/5 tbsp boiling water
10ml/2 tsp coffee and chicory essence

For the toffee sauce

75g/3oz/6 tbsp light muscovado
   (brown) sugar
50g/2oz/¼ cup butter
60ml/4 tbsp double (heavy) cream
30ml/2 tbsp brandy

1 Preheat the oven to 180°C/350°F/ Gas 4. Place a baking sheet in the oven. Grease six pudding moulds.

2 Cream the butter and sugar in a large mixing bowl until pale and fluffy. Gradually add the beaten eggs a little at a time, beating well after each addition.

3 Sift the flour and bicarbonate of soda together and fold into the creamed mixture.

4 Put the dates in a heatproof bowl, pour over the boiling water and mash with a potato masher. Add the coffee and chicory essence, then stir the paste into the creamed mixture.

COOK'S TIP

It is preferable to peel the dates as the skins can be rather tough: simply squeeze them between your thumb and forefinger and the skins will pop off.

5 Spoon the mixture into the prepared moulds. Place on the hot baking sheet and bake for 20 minutes.

6 To make the toffee sauce, put all the ingredients in a pan and heat gently, stirring until smooth.

7 Increase the heat and boil for 1 minute. Turn the warm puddings out on to individual dessert plates. Spoon a generous amount of sauce over each and serve immediately.

Berry Sauce with Baked Ricotta Cakes

THE FLAVOUR OF THIS fragrant fruity sauce contrasts well with these honey and vanilla-flavoured desserts.

Serves 4

INGREDIENTS

250g/9oz/generous 1 cup ricotta cheese
2 egg whites, beaten
about 60ml/4 tbsp clear honey
few drops of vanilla essence (extract)
fresh mint leaves, to decorate (optional)

For the red berry sauce

450g/1lb/4 cups mixed fresh or frozen fruit, such as strawberries, raspberries, blackberries and cherries

COOK'S TIPS

• *The sauce can be made a day ahead. Chill until ready to use.*
• *Frozen fruit doesn't need extra water, as there will be ice crystals clinging to the berries.*

1 Preheat the oven to 180°C/350°F/ Gas 4.

2 Place the ricotta cheese in a bowl and break it up with a wooden spoon. Add the beaten egg whites, honey and vanilla essence and mix thoroughly until the mixture is smooth and well combined.

3 Lightly grease four ramekins. Spoon the ricotta mixture into the prepared ramekins and level the tops. Bake for 20 minutes or until the ricotta cakes are risen and golden.

4 Meanwhile, make the berry sauce. Reserve about one-quarter of the fruit for decoration. Place the rest of the fruit in a pan, with a little water if using fresh fruit, and heat gently until softened. Leave to cool slightly. Remove any cherry pits, if using.

5 Press the fruit through a sieve, then taste and sweeten with honey if it is too tart. Serve the sauce, warm or cold, with the ricotta cakes. Decorate with the reserved berries and mint leaves, if using.

Calvados and Chocolate Sauce with Iced Pear Terrine

THIS RICH CHOCOLATE SAUCE would complement vanilla ice cream for a simpler dessert.

Serves 8

INGREDIENTS

1.3–1.6kg/3–3½ lb ripe Williams pears
juice of 1 lemon
115g/4oz/½ cup caster (superfine) sugar
10 whole cloves
julienne strips of orange rind, to decorate

For the Calvados and chocolate sauce
200g/7oz plain (semisweet) chocolate
60ml/4 tbsp hot strong black coffee
200ml/7fl oz/1 cup double (heavy) cream
30ml/2 tbsp Calvados or brandy

1 Peel, core and slice the pears. Place in a pan with the lemon juice, sugar, cloves and 90ml/6 tbsp water. Cover and simmer for 10 minutes. Remove the cloves. Allow to cool.

2 Process the pears with their juice and pour the purée into a freezer-proof bowl. Cover and freeze until firm.

3 Line a 900g/2lb loaf tin (pan) with clear film (plastic wrap). Allow the film to overhang the sides of the tin. Remove the frozen pear purée from the freezer and spoon it into a food processor. Process until smooth. Pour into the prepared tin, cover and freeze until firm.

4 To make the sauce, break the chocolate into a large, heatproof bowl. Place the bowl over a pan of hot water and allow to melt.

5 Stir the coffee into the melted chocolate until smooth. Gradually stir in the cream and then the Calvados or brandy. Set aside.

6 About 20 minutes before serving, remove the tin from the freezer. Invert the terrine on to a plate, lift off the clear film and place the terrine in the refrigerator to soften slightly. Warm the sauce over hot water.

7 Place a slice of terrine on to each dessert plate and spoon over some of the sauce. Decorate with julienne strips of orange rind and serve immediately.

COOK'S TIP

This is a good dish to prepare in advance for a dinner party, as the terrine will store successfully for a month in the freezer, but remember to remove it in time to soften slightly before serving.

Mexican Hot Fudge Sauce with Sundaes

DEFINITELY NOT ONE FOR dieters, but best kept for those indulgent days!

Serves 4

INGREDIENTS
600ml/1 pint/2½ cups vanilla ice cream
600ml/1 pint/2½ cups coffee ice cream
2 large ripe bananas, sliced
whipped cream
toasted flaked (sliced) almonds

For the hot fudge sauce
60ml/4 tbsp muscovado (molasses) sugar
115g/4oz/⅓ cup golden (light corn) syrup
45ml/3 tbsp strong black coffee
5ml/1 tsp ground cinnamon
150g/5oz dark (bittersweet) chocolate, broken up
75ml/5 tbsp whipping cream
45ml/3 tbsp coffee liqueur (optional)

1 For the sauce, combine the sugar, golden syrup, coffee and cinnamon in a heavy pan. Bring to the boil. Boil the mixture, stirring constantly, for about 5 minutes.

COOK'S TIP

Use a good quality, plain dark chocolate with at least 70 per cent cocoa solids.

2 Remove from the heat and stir in the chocolate. When melted and smooth, stir in the cream and liqueur, if using. Let the sauce cool just to lukewarm, or if made ahead, reheat gently while assembling the sundaes.

3 Using an ice-cream scoop, fill the sundae dishes with one scoop each of vanilla and coffee ice cream.

4 Arrange the bananas on the top of each dish. Pour the warm sauce over the bananas.

5 Top each sundae with a generous rosette of whipped cream. Top with the toasted almonds and serve immediately.

Sabayon Sauce

THIS FROTHY SAUCE is very versatile and can be served alone or hot over cake, fruit or even ice cream. Never let the sauce stand before serving, as it will collapse.

Serves 4–6

INGREDIENTS

1 egg

2 egg yolks

75g/3oz/scant ½ cup caster (superfine) sugar

150ml/¼ pint/⅔ cup Marsala or other sweet white wine

finely grated rind and juice of 1 lemon

dessert biscuits (cookies), to serve

1 Put the egg, yolks and sugar into a medium bowl and whisk until they are pale and thick.

2 Stand the bowl over a pan of hot, but not boiling, water. Gradually add the Marsala or white wine and lemon juice, a little at a time, whisking vigorously.

3 Continue whisking until it is thick enough to leave a trail.

COOK'S TIP

A generous pinch of arrowroot whisked together with the egg yolks and sugar will prevent the sauce collapsing too quickly.

4 To serve the sabayon cold, place it over a bowl of iced water and continue whisking until chilled. Add the finely grated lemon rind and stir in. Pour into small glasses and serve immediately, with the dessert biscuits.

Chocolate Sauce with Profiteroles

A REAL TREAT IF you're not counting calories, this sauce is also good with scoops of vanilla ice cream.

Serves 6

INGREDIENTS

65g/2½oz/9 tbsp plain (all-purpose) flour
50g/2oz/¼ cup butter
150ml/¼ pint/⅔ cup water
2 eggs, lightly beaten
150ml/¼ pint/⅔ cup whipping
    cream, whipped

For the chocolate sauce

150ml/¼ pint/⅔ cup double (heavy) cream
50g/2oz/¼ cup butter
50g/2oz/¼ cup vanilla sugar
175g/6oz plain (semisweet) chocolate
30ml/2 tbsp brandy

VARIATION

White chocolate and orange sauce
40g/1½oz/3 tbsp caster (superfine) sugar,
    to replace vanilla sugar
finely grated rind of 1 orange
175g/6oz white chocolate, to replace
    plain (semisweet) chocolate
30ml/2 tbsp orange liqueur, to
    replace brandy

1 Make the chocolate sauce. Heat the cream with the butter and vanilla sugar in a bowl over a pan of hot, but not boiling water. Stir until smooth, then cool.

2 Break the chocolate into the cream. Stir until it is melted and thoroughly combined.

3 Stir in the brandy a little at a time, then leave the sauce to cool to room temperature.

4 For the white chocolate and orange sauce, heat the cream and butter with the caster sugar and orange rind in the top of a double boiler, until dissolved. Use the white chocolate instead of plain chocolate in step 2, and orange liqueur instead of the brandy in step 3.

5 To make the profiteroles, preheat the oven to 200°C/400°F/Gas 6. Sift the flour on to a plate. Melt the butter and water in a pan and bring to the boil.

6 Remove the pan from the heat and tip the flour in all at once. Beat with a wooden spoon until smooth. Cool for 1–2 minutes, then gradually beat in enough egg to give a piping consistency. Beat well until glossy. Pipe small balls of the mixture on to dampened baking sheets.

7 Bake in the oven for 15–20 minutes, or until crisp. Make a slit in the sides and cool on a wire rack.

8 Fill a piping (pastry) bag with cream and pipe some into each profiterole. Pile on to a plate, topped with a little sauce. Serve the remaining chocolate sauce separately.

Papaya Sauce with Grilled Pineapple

TRY THE PAPAYA SAUCE with savoury dishes, too. It tastes great with grilled chicken and game birds as well as pork and lamb.

Serves 6

INGREDIENTS

1 sweet pineapple

melted butter, for greasing and brushing

2 pieces drained stem (crystallized) ginger in syrup, cut into fine matchsticks, plus 30ml/2 tsp syrup

30ml/2 tbsp demerara (raw) sugar

pinch of ground cinnamon

fresh mint sprigs, to decorate

For the papaya sauce

1 ripe papaya, peeled and seeded

175ml/6fl oz/¾ cup apple juice

1 Peel the pineapple and take spiral slices off the outside to remove the eyes. Cut it crossways into six slices, each 2.5cm/1in thick.

2 Line a baking sheet with a sheet of foil, rolling up the sides to make a rim. Grease the foil with melted butter. Preheat the grill (broiler).

VARIATION

If you like, substitute half apple juice and half papaya nectar for the apple juice in the sauce.

3 Arrange the pineapple slices on the baking sheet. Brush with butter, then top with ginger, sugar and cinnamon. Drizzle over the ginger syrup. Grill (broil) for 5–7 minutes, until the slices are lightly charred.

4 Cut a few slices from the papaya and set aside, then purée the rest together with the apple juice in a food processor or blender.

5 Press the purée through a sieve placed over a bowl, then stir in any juices from cooking the pineapple.

6 Serve the pineapple slices with a little sauce drizzled around each plate. Decorate with the reserved papaya slices and the mint sprigs.

Nectarine Sauce with Latticed Peaches

MAKE THIS IN SUMMER when the fruits are in season, and enjoy the fresh flavour.

Serves 6

INGREDIENTS

For the pastry
115g/4oz/1 cup plain (all-purpose) flour
45ml/3 tbsp butter
45ml/3 tbsp natural (plain) yogurt
30ml/2 tbsp orange juice
milk, for brushing

For the filling
3 ripe peaches or nectarines
45ml/3 tbsp ground almonds
30ml/2 tbsp low-fat natural (plain) yogurt
finely grated rind of 1 small orange
1.5ml/¼ tsp almond essence (extract)

For the nectarine sauce
1 ripe nectarine or peach
45ml/3 tbsp orange juice

1 For the pastry, sift the flour into a bowl and, using your fingertips, rub in the butter. Stir in the yogurt and orange juice to bind the mixture to a firm dough.

2 Roll out about half the pastry thinly, and use a pastry cutter to stamp out rounds of about 7.5cm/3in in diameter, or slightly larger than the circumference of the peaches. Place on a lightly greased baking sheet.

3 Skin, halve and stone (pit) the peaches or nectarines.

4 Mix together the almonds, yogurt, orange rind and almond essence. Spoon into each fruit half and place, cut-side down, on the pastry rounds.

5 Roll out the remaining pastry thinly and cut into thin strips. Arrange the strips over the peaches to form a lattice, brushing with milk to secure firmly. Trim off the ends neatly.

6 Chill in the refrigerator for 30 minutes. Preheat the oven to 200°C/400°F/Gas 6. Brush the tarts with milk, and bake for 15–18 minutes.

7 For the sauce, skin the nectarine or peach and remove the stone (pit). Purée it in a food processor, with the orange juice. Serve the peaches hot, with the sauce spooned around.

COOK'S TIP

To peel peaches, blanch them in boiling water for about 30 seconds then place in iced water. The skins will slip off.

Lime and Cardamom Sauce with Bananas

THE WARM FLAVOUR of cardamom is offset by the tang of lime.

Serves 4

INGREDIENTS
6 small bananas
25g/1oz/2 tbsp butter
vanilla ice cream, to serve

For the lime and cardamom sauce
25g/1oz/2 tbsp butter
seeds from 4 cardamom pods, crushed
50g/2oz/½ cup flaked (sliced) almonds
thinly pared rind and juice of 2 limes
50g/2oz/¼ cup light muscovado
   (brown) sugar
30ml/2 tbsp dark rum

1 Peel the bananas and cut them in half lengthways. Heat the butter in a large frying pan. Add half the bananas, and cook until the undersides are golden. Turn carefully, using a fish slice (spatula).

2 As they cook, transfer the bananas to a heatproof serving dish. Cook the remaining bananas in the same way.

VARIATION

If you prefer not to use alcohol in your cooking, replace the rum with orange juice or even pineapple juice.

3 To make the lime and cardamom sauce melt the butter, then add the cardamom seeds and almonds. Cook, stirring, until golden.

4 Stir in the lime rind and juice, then the sugar. Cook, stirring, until the mixture is smooth, bubbling and slightly reduced. Stir in the rum.

5 Pour the sauce over the bananas and serve immediately, with vanilla ice cream.

COOK'S TIP

Crush the cardamom seeds in a mortar and pestle just before using, to retain their essential flavour.

Maple Yogurt Sauce with Poached Pears

THE SWEET-SOUR TASTE OF the maple syrup and yogurt will partner most poached fruit but is especially good with pears. Choose a firm but ripe pear such as Conference.

Serves 4

INGREDIENTS

4 firm dessert pears
15ml/1 tbsp lemon juice
250ml/8fl oz/1 cup sweet white wine
thinly pared rind of 1 lemon
1 cinnamon stick

For the maple yogurt sauce

pear cooking liquid
30ml/2 tbsp maple syrup
2.5ml/½ tsp arrowroot
150g/5oz/⅔ cup Greek (US strained plain) yogurt

1 Thinly peel the pears, leaving them whole and with stalks. Brush them with lemon juice, to prevent them from browning. Use a potato peeler or small knife to scoop out the core from the base of each pear.

2 Place the pears in a wide, heavy pan and pour the wine over them, with enough cold water almost to cover the pears.

3 Add the lemon rind and cinnamon stick and bring to the boil. Reduce the heat, cover the pan and simmer gently for 30–40 minutes, or until the pears are tender. Turn the pears occasionally so that they cook evenly. Lift them out carefully, draining them.

4 To make the sauce, bring the liquid to the boil and boil uncovered to reduce it to about 105ml/7 tbsp. Strain and add the maple syrup. Blend a little with the arrowroot. Return to the pan and cook, stirring, until thick. Cool.

5 Slice each cored pear about three-quarters of the way through, leaving the slices attached at the stem end. Fan out on a serving plate.

6 Stir 30ml/2 tbsp of the cooled syrup into the yogurt and spoon it around the pears. Drizzle with the remaining syrup and serve immediately.

VARIATION

If you want to make this sauce for another dessert, substitute fruit juice for the pear cooking liquid in step 4.

Strawberry Sauce with Lemon Hearts

THIS SPEEDY SWEET SAUCE makes a delicious accompaniment for these delicate lemon and cheese hearts.

Serves 4

INGREDIENTS

175g/6oz/¾ cup ricotta cheese
150ml/¼ pint/⅔ cup natural (plain) yogurt
15ml/1 tbsp sugar
finely grated rind of ½ lemon
30ml/2 tbsp lemon juice
10ml/2 tsp powdered gelatine
2 egg whites
oil, for greasing

For the strawberry sauce
225g/8oz/2 cups fresh or frozen and
   thawed strawberries, plus extra
   to decorate
15ml/1 tbsp lemon juice

1 Beat the ricotta until smooth. Stir in the yogurt, sugar and lemon rind.

2 Place the lemon juice in a small bowl and sprinkle the gelatine over it. Place the bowl over a pan of hot water and stir the mixture to dissolve the gelatine completely.

3 Beat the egg whites until they form soft peaks. Quickly stir the gelatine into the ricotta cheese mixture, mixing it in evenly, then immediately fold in the beaten egg whites.

4 Spoon the mixture into four lightly oiled, individual heart-shaped moulds and chill the moulds until set.

5 To make the sauce, place the strawberries and lemon juice in a food processor and process until smooth. Pour on to plates and top with turned-out hearts. Decorate with the extra strawberries.

VARIATION

Add a dash of Cointreau or Grand Marnier liqueur to the strawberry sauce.

Index

all-in-one method 29
apple sauce 61
    and creamy Calvados 96
arrowroot 11
avocado sauce 88

baked custard 37
baked fish with tahini sauce 115
baked marrow and parsley
    sauce 129
banana:
    and malted chocolate dip with
        fresh fruit 139
    with lime and cardamom
        sauce 155
barbecue sauce 60
béarnaise sauce 53
béchamel sauce 44
beef: and broccoli stir-fry with
        black bean sauce 104
    Roquefort and walnut butter
        with rump steak 105
    stock 26
berry sauce with baked ricotta
    cakes 148
beurre blanc 34
beurre manié 29
black bean: and five-spice sauce
        with stir-fried squid 122
    sauce with beef and broccoli
        stir-fry 104
black forest sauce 38

blending method 28
blue cheese and walnut sauce 57
bolognese sauce 77
bread sauce 63
bream, sea, with orange butter
    sauce 114
brown sauce 30, 31
butter: and herb sauce 76
    clarifying 35
    flavoured 35
    orange butter sauce 114
    sauce 120
    savoury sauces 34
butterscotch sauce 39, 143

Calvados: and apple sauce 96
    and chocolate sauce 149
cannelloni with two sauces 70
carbonara sauce 72

cardamom and lime sauce with
    bananas 155
castle puddings with real
    custard 146
cauliflower with cheddar
    cheese sauce 134
choron sauce 53
chasseur sauce 49
cheddar see cheeses
cheeses 22
    berry sauce with baked
        ricotta cakes 148
    blue cheese and walnut
        sauce 57
    cheddar cheese sauce with
        cauliflower 134
    cheese and ham ravioli 67
    cheese sauce 45
    gorgonzola sauce 73
    parmesan and cream sauce 74
    quick tomato sauce with
        baked cheese polenta 131
    Roquefort and walnut butter
        with rump steak 105
    smoked cheese sauce with
        veal escalopes 99
    strawberry sauce with lemon
        hearts 157
    vermouth and chèvre sauce
        with pan-fried cod 110
    wild mushroom sauce with
        polenta and gorgonzola 135
chèvre and vermouth sauce
    with pan-fried cod 11
chicken: avocado sauce with
        lemon chicken 88
    enchiladas with salsa picante
        90
    stock 26
chilli: and tomato sauce 68
    barbecue sauce with
        salmon 119
    -nectarine relish 97
chocolate sauce 41
    and Calvados 149
    chocolate-toffee sauce 38
    malted chocolate and banana
        dip with fresh fruit 139
    with profiteroles 152
citrus sauce with baby
    courgettes 127
classic sauces: apple 61
    barbecue 60
    basic white 45
    béarnaise 53
    béchamel 44
    blue cheese and walnut 57
    bread 63
    chasseur 49
    cheese 45
    cranberry 62
    Espagnole 48
    green peppercorn 59

hollandaise 34, 51
horseradish 63
lemon with tarragon 47
mint 62
mousseline 52
newburg 54
parsley 45, 109, 129
pesto 16–17, 55
quick satay 58
rich tomato 56
tangy orange 39, 50
velouté 46
coconut milk/cream 17
cod, pan-fried, with vermouth
    and chèvre sauce 110
Cointreau and maple syrup
    with oranges 144
cornflour 11
coulis: fruit 40, 140
    tomato 116
courgette: and tomato sauce 71
    with citrus sauce 127
crab cakes with tartare
    sauce 123
cranberry sauce 62
    with venison 102
creams 20
    cream and parmesan sauce 74
    cream and walnut sauce 78
    Marsala cream sauce with
        turkey 91
    smoked salmon and cream
        sauce 82
crème anglaise 37
    chocolate 41
crème fraîche 20–21
crêpe sauces 39
Cumberland sauce with
    gammon 101
custard: 37
    chocolate 41
    powder 11
    with castle puddings 146

dairy products 20–22
date puddings with toffee
    sauce 147
deglazed sauces 31
dessert sauces see sweet dishes
dill and mustard sauce with
    sole 111
duck breasts with walnut and
    pomegranate sauce 92

egg sauces: savoury 36
    sweet 37
eggs 22
    egg yolk liaison 29
    sauces 36, 37
equipment 23–25
Espagnole sauce 48
essences 19

fats 12–14
fish dishes: butter sauce with
        salmon cakes 120
    chilli barbecue sauce with
        salmon 119

dill and mustard sauce
    with sole 111
with stir-fried squid 122
gooseberry sauce with
    mackerel 112
herb sauce with sardines 113
orange and caper sauce
    with skate 108
orange butter sauce with sea
    bream 114
parsley sauce with haddock
    109
seafood with warm green
    tartare sauce 121
smoked haddock and
    parsley 81
smoked salmon and cream 82
sorrel sauce with salmon
    steaks 118
tahini sauce with baked
    fish 115
tartare sauce with crab
    cakes 123
tomato coulis with
    marinated monkfish 116
vermouth and chèvre sauce
    with pan-fried cod 110
fish stock 26
five-spice and black bean sauce
    with stir-fried squid 122
flour-based sauces 28–31
flours 10–11
flower waters 19
fruit sauces 40
    apple 61
    berry 148
    chilli-nectarine relish 97
    cranberry 62, 102
    creamy Calvados and
        apple 96
    gooseberry sauce 112
    hot plum 145
    lemon and lime 142
    lime and cardamom 155

malted chocolate and
banana 139
nectarine 154
orange 39, 50
orange and caper 108
orange butter 114
papaya 153
papaya dip 138
passion fruit coulis 40, 140
peach 40
redcurrant 93
strawberry 157
summer berry 39
walnut and pomegranate 92
fudge sauce, hot, with
sundaes 150

gammon with Cumberland
sauce 101
ginger and tomato sauce with
tofu and potato rösti 132
gnocchi with gorgonzola
sauce 73
goat's cheese and vermouth
sauce with pan-fried cod 110
gooseberry sauce with
mackerel 112
gorgonzola: and polenta with
wild mushroom sauce 135
gravy 31
green peppercorn sauce 59
green vegetable sauce 126

haddock and parsley sauce
81, 109
ham and cheese ravioli 67
hazelnut dip with fruit
fondue 140
herbs 18
butter and herb sauce 76
sorrel sauce with salmon
steaks 118
with sardines 113
hollandaise 34, 51
horseradish sauce 63
hot date puddings with toffee
sauce 147
hot fudge sauce with
sundaes 150
hot plum sauce with floating
islands 145

ice cream toppings 38
Italian plum tomato sauce 67

lamb: burgers with redcurrant
sauce 93
roast leg with pesto 95
tomato sauce with Greek
lamb sausages 94
lemon: and lime sauce with
pancakes 142
chicken with avocado
sauce 88

hearts with strawberry
sauce 157
sauce with tarragon 47
lime: and cardamom sauce with
bananas 155
and lemon sauce with
pancakes 142
lumpy sauce, correcting 30

mackerel with gooseberry
sauce 112
malfatti with roasted pepper
sauce 130
malted chocolate and banana
dip with fresh fruit 139

maple yogurt sauce with
poached pears 156
marinated monkfish with
tomato coulis 116
marmalade whisky sauce 38
marrow, baked, and parsley
sauce 129
Marsala cream sauce with
turkey 91
marshmallow melt 38
mayonnaise 36
meat dishes: avocado with
lemon chicken 88
black bean sauce with beef
and broccoli stir-fry 104
chilli-nectarine relish with
pork chops 97
cranberry sauce with
venison 102
gammon with Cumberland
sauce 101
Marsala cream sauce with
turkey 91
noisettes of pork with creamy
Calvados and apple 96
pesto with roast leg of
lamb 95
redcurrant sauce with lamb
burgers 93
Roquefort and walnut butter
with rump steak 105
sage and orange sauce with
pork fillet 98
salsa picante with chicken
enchiladas 90
smoked cheese sauce with
veal escalopes 99

sweet-and-sour sauce with
pork 100
tomato sauce with Greek
lamb sausages 94
walnut and pomegranate
sauce with duck breasts 92
Mexican hot fudge sauce
with sundaes 150
milk 20
mint sauce 62
monkfish, marinated, with
tomato coulis 116
mousseline sauce 52
mushroom sauce 85, 135
mustards 16
dill and mustard sauce
with sole 111

nectarine: chilli relish 97
sauce with latticed peaches
154
newburg sauce 54
noisettes of pork with creamy
Calvados and apple 96
Normandy apple sauce 61

oils 12–14
orange sauce 39, 50
and sage 98
orange butter sauce 114
with capers 108
oranges with maple and
Cointreau syrup 144
oyster sauce, commercial 16

pancakes with lemon and
lime sauce 142
pans 23–24
pansotti 78
papaya: dip with fresh fruit 138
sauce with grilled pineapple
153
parmesan and cream sauce 74
parsley sauce 45, 109, 129
passion fruit coulis 40, 140
pasta 66
cheese and ham ravioli 67
gnocchi 73
pansotti 78
ravioli 77
seafood shells 80
spinach and ricotta ravioli 74
pasta sauces: bolognese 77
butter and herb 76
cannelloni with two sauces 70
carbonara 72
cream and parmesan 74
cream and walnut 78
gorgonzola 73
green vegetable 126
Italian plum tomato 67
prawn and vodka 82
smoked haddock and
parsley 81

smoked salmon and cream 82
spicy sausage 84
spinach 80
sun-dried tomato and
radicchio 69
tomato and chilli 68
tomato and courgette 71
wild mushroom 85
peach: latticed, with nectarine
sauce 154
sauce 40
peanuts: quick satay sauce 58
sauce with warm vegetable
salad 128
pear: poached, with maple
yogurt sauce 156
terrine, iced, with Calvados
and chocolate sauce 149
pepper sauces, commercial 16
peppercorn sauce, green 59
pesto: commercial 16–17
home-made 55
with roast leg of lamb 95
pineapple, grilled, with papaya
sauce 153
plum sauce, hot, with floating
islands 145
polenta: and gorgonzola with
wild mushroom sauce 135
baked cheese, with quick
tomato sauce 131
pomegranate and walnut
sauce 92
pork: chops with chilli-nectarine
relish 97
fillet, with sage and orange
sauce 98
noisettes, with creamy
Calvados and apple sauce 96

with sweet-and-sour
sauce 100
potato flour 11
potato rösti and tofu with
tomato and ginger sauce 132
prawn and vodka sauce 82
presentation 39
profiteroles with chocolate
sauce 152

quick satay sauce 58
quick tomato sauce with
baked cheese polenta 131

radicchio and sun-dried
    tomato 69
ravioli 77
    cheese and ham 67
    spinach and ricotta 74
redcurrant sauce 93
rich butterscotch sauce 39
rich tomato sauce 56
ricotta: and spinach ravioli with
    cream and parmesan sauce 74
    baked ricotta cakes with
        berry sauce 148
    strawberry sauce with lemon
        hearts 157
roast leg of lamb with pesto 95
roasted pepper sauce with
    malfatti 130
roasted vegetable sauce 33
Roquefort and walnut butter
    with rump steak 105
roux method 28, 30

sabayon sauce 37, 151
sage and orange sauce with pork
    fillet 98
salmon: cakes with butter
    sauce 120
    smoked, and cream sauce 82
    steaks with sorrel sauce 118
    with chilli barbecue sauce 119
salsa: crudo 32
    picante with chicken
        enchiladas 90
sardines with herb sauce 113
satay sauce 58
sauce bigarade 50
sausage sauce, spicy 84
savoury butter: 35
    sauces 34
scallops with warm green
    tartare sauce 121
sea bream with orange butter
    sauce 114

seafood: pasta shells with
    spinach sauce 80
    with warm green tartare
        sauce 121
skate with orange and caper
    sauce 108
smoked cheese sauce with
    veal escalopes 99

smoked haddock and parsley
    sauce 81
smoked salmon and cream
    sauce 82
sole with dill and mustard
    sauce 111
sorrel sauce with salmon
    steaks 118
soy sauce 17
spices 19
spicy sausage sauce 84
spinach: and ricotta ravioli with
    cream and parmesan sauce 74
    malfatti with roasted pepper
        sauce 130
squid, stir-fried, with five-spice
    and black bean sauce 122
steak see beef
stir-fried squid with five-spice
    and black bean sauce 122
stock: cubes/powders 15
    home-made 26
    keeping clear 27
    removing fat 27
    storing 27
strawberry sauce with lemon
    hearts 157
summer berry sauce 39
sun-dried tomato and radicchio
    sauce 69
sweet-and-sour sauce with
    pork 100
sweet dishes 38–39
    berry sauce with baked
        ricotta cakes 148
    butterscotch sauce with
        waffles 143
    Calvados and chocolate sauce
        with iced pear terrine 149
    chocolate sauce with
        profiteroles 152
    hazelnut dip with fruit
        fondue 140
    hot plum sauce with floating
        islands 145
    lemon and lime sauce with
        pancakes 142
    lime and cardamom sauce
        with bananas 155
    malted chocolate and banana
        dip with fresh fruit 139
    maple and Cointreau syrup
        with oranges 144
    maple yogurt sauce with
        poached pears 156
    Mexican hot fudge sauce
        with sundaes 150
    nectarine sauce with latticed
        peaches 154
    papaya dip with fresh fruit 138
    papaya sauce with grilled
        pineapple 153
    passion fruit coulis with
        yogurt sundaes 140

real custard with castle
    puddings 146
strawberry sauce with lemon
    hearts 157
toffee sauce with hot date
    puddings 147
sweet egg sauces 37

tahini sauce with baked fish 115
tangy orange sauce 50

tartare sauce: warm green, with
    seafood 121
    with crab cakes 123
Thai fish sauce, commercial 17
toffee sauce with hot date
    puddings 147
tofu and potato rösti with
    tomato and ginger sauce 132
tomato: and chilli sauce 68
    and courgette sauce 71
    basic sauce 32
    canned 15–16
    chilli barbecue sauce 119
    coulis with marinated
        monkfish 116
    how to peel 33
    Italian plum tomato sauce 67
    quick tomato sauce with
        baked cheese polenta 131
    rich sauce 56
    sauce with Greek lamb
        sausages 94
    sun-dried tomato and
        radicchio sauce 69
turkey with Marsala cream
    sauce 91

vanilla pods 38
veal escalopes with smoked
    cheese sauce 99
vegetable salad, warm, with
    peanut sauce 128
vegetable sauces 32–33
    green 126
    roasted pepper sauce with
        malfatti 130
vegetable stock 26
vegetarian dishes: baked
    marrow and parsley
        sauce 129
    cheddar cheese sauce with
        cauliflower 134

citrus sauce with baby
    courgettes 127
fresh tomato and ginger
    sauce with tofu and potato
    rösti 132
green vegetable 126
peanut sauce with warm
    vegetable salad 128
quick tomato sauce with
    baked cheese polenta 131
roasted pepper sauce with
    malfatti 130
wild mushroom sauce with
    polenta and gorgonzola 135
velouté sauce 46
venison with cranberry sauce
    102
vermouth and chèvre sauce
    with pan-fried cod 110
vinegars 17
vodka and prawn sauce 82

waffles with butterscotch sauce
    143
walnut: and blue cheese sauce
    57
    and cream sauce 78
    and pomegranate sauce 92
    and Roquefort butter with
        rump steak 105
warm green tartare sauce 121
warm vegetable salad with
    peanut sauce 128
whisky sauce 38
white sauces 28–30, 45
wild mushroom sauce 85, 135
Worcestershire sauce 17

yogurt 21
    maple yogurt sauce with
        poached pears 156
    sundaes with passion fruit
        coulis 140